Jane Peyton

summersdale

BRILLIANT BRITAIN

Summersdale Publishers Ltd
46 West Street
Chichester
West Sussex
PO19 1RP
UK

www.summersdale.com

Printed and bound in Great Britain

ISBN: 978-1-84024-706-0

Disclaimer
Every effort has been made to attribute the quotations in this collection to the correct source. Should there be any omissions or errors in this respect we apologise and shall be pleased to make the appropriate acknowledgements in any future editions.

For my dad Bill, who was a brilliant Briton

Contents

Acknowledgements

Thank you very much to everyone who answered my research questions, and to the vicar of All Hallows-by-the-Tower, the committee of the Dunmow Flitch Trials, and Historic Royal Palaces (Tower of London) for permitting me to use extended quotes and dialogue. Thanks to Steve Roud for writing such an interesting book called *The English Year* (published by Penguin) that I read during my research. And thanks also to the team at Summersdale; to Caragh Hanning for Rosebank; Emma, James, Eleanor and Alice for cuckoo and cake; Kevin Haug and Gail Willumsen for the envelope; to my siblings who are lovely, and to everyone in my life who is brilliant.

Author's Note

I was born in North Yorkshire and currently reside in London, but lived for a while in the US and New Zealand, where official historical records date back only four centuries. Their cultures had nothing to equal the out-of-the-ordinary traditions that I took for granted in Britain. Whilst based in Los Angeles, California, I would often see signs that proudly proclaimed businesses as being 'Established in 1973'. In the US, Britons were perceived as eccentric. It was not meant pejoratively, but was rather an affectionate description of a race of individuals who had a good sense of humour, and who were certainly not bland.

When I was away I missed countless things about Britain, not least the self-deprecating wit, a celebration of the ridiculous, a tendency not to take one's self too seriously, an ability to find the fun in a situation, and the Shipping Forecast (it was before Internet radio). I started thinking of all the wonderfully batty events that happen around the country – gurning championships are a particular favourite – and then realised that if a Hollywood film were ever made about British traditions no one outside the British Isles would believe they were true. Maybe not even Britons themselves!

It was hard to choose which traditions and rituals to include within these pages – my selection is certainly not exhaustive, but it does reflect the wide, and sometimes wild, variety of British customs. The State Opening of Parliament is a solemn spectacle, the ultimate in pomp and ceremony, whilst Flora Day in Helston, when dance fever infects the entire town, is delightfully festive, and Well Dressing, where water is revered with exquisite floral tributes, is a charming communal event. Delving into the accents, dialects and slang of the English language was a fascinating experience: English is so playful, entertaining, alive and inclusive – it has never met a word that is not welcome in the lexicon.

If I had to sum up the British in one line it would be: they like to dress up, dance, drink and dabble in daft sports. Amen.

Jane Peyton

Introduction

Britain is unique. One reason is its customs. It is a nation that cares deeply about heritage, traditions and rituals – especially if any of these involve dressing up in costume, participating in slightly bonkers pastimes and going down the pub.

Any concerns about globalisation turning Britain into a homogenous land with no local character should be quelled by reading this book. Whether they're charming worms from the soil or playing cricket on a sandbar that rises from the sea only once a year, there is no doubt that Britons belong to a culture that is one of a kind.

One thing that struck me during my research was that whilst the rituals and traditions are diverse, the participants share some common traits:

 They really join in the spirit of the activity: 'No problem, I'll wear a mask, ride backwards on that donkey and agree to fall off it a few times. Oh, and get us another pint while you're at the bar will you, mate?'

 Their tongues are firmly in their cheeks: 'And now, please welcome the trainer of this year's world champion racing snail!'

Their attitude can be very matter of fact: 'Oh look, there's a man dressed up as a straw dancing bear. Anyway, what were you saying about the bus being late?'

Some of them don't quite know why they take part, but no matter. Their predecessors did it, so they give it a go too; even if that means getting out of bed before dawn in winter to deposit a few pennies on a stone at the top of a hill.

There is no sense of 'Aren't we wacky?': people participate wholeheartedly, as though it is commonplace to gather in an orchard, hang pieces of toast from an apple tree and pour cider on its roots.

As I learned more about the heritage of these customs, I discovered several recurring factors. The provenance of rituals is often shrouded in mystery and contradiction. In many cases there are no written records about their origins and no one can explain why they are practised, so imaginative legends have been devised instead. There were a number of traditions that were alleged to date back over a thousand years, being pagan or related to medieval fertility rites. These often turned out to have been practices invented in the eighteenth or nineteenth century and given a fake history.

Land rights is another theme that kept cropping up, and how the 'people' had fought for the right to graze animals on or collect wood from land that had been obtained by, or assigned to, a favourite of the king. Several customs in this book were initiated to commemorate these hard-won privileges.

The customs cannot all boast an uninterrupted history, usually because they have been banned at some point by killjoy Puritans under Oliver Cromwell or straight-laced Victorians. The Puritans wanted to proscribe anything that was not sober and did not have a prayer book in its hand. Victorians prohibited events where public drunkenness got out of hand (they were kept very busy) or anything deemed too anarchic at that dour time. Thankfully, many of these suppressed practices were revived in the twentieth century and still take place today.

This book focuses on traditions and events that occur throughout the year that are unusual, sometimes eccentric, but above all fun and thoroughly British. The history behind the traditions and a detailed description of how the custom or ritual is performed might inspire readers to explore and visit them in person. Most of the events are public, and welcome spectators and entrants – the majority have websites for more information and if not, local tourist offices will advise on when and where they take place. Everything featured – be that competitive black pudding throwing or snorkelling through a bog – is utterly brilliant.

Festivals and Pageants

Few towns and villages throughout the British Isles choose not to stage an annual fair, fete or seasonal celebration. Some are simple fiestas to raise funds for the village hall whilst others are extravaganzas that take months of preparation. They vary between the foolhardy (swinging fireballs around the head to celebrate Hogmanay), the boisterous (morris dancing and unforgettable costumes) and the exquisite (adorning wells with flowers in thanks for the water). The events included in the following chapter are amongst the most spectacular.

On Fire

Bonfire Night, countrywide

Remember, remember the fifth of November
Gunpowder, treason and plot
I see no reason why gunpowder treason
Should ever be forgot.

Satellite images of Britain on 5 November reveal a country in flames. Or so it might seem as thousands of bonfires burn and fireworks explode to commemorate the actions of Guy Fawkes and his thwarted attempt to blow up the Palace of Westminster. Guy Fawkes was a member of a group who conspired to kill King James I and the government during the State Opening of Parliament in 1605.

The plotters rented a cellar beneath the House of Lords where they stashed 36 barrels (815 kilograms) of gunpowder. Guy, or Guido as he was also known, was an explosives expert assigned the task of detonating the bombs. But the plot was foiled because one of the conspirators sent a warning letter to a member of the House of Lords (a Catholic, like the plotters). Just as Guy was about to light the fuse he was grabbed by guards. The gang was sentenced to be hung, drawn and quartered, a brutal mode of execution reserved for those found guilty of high treason. The prisoners were hung by the neck for a short time, disembowelled (their entrails burned in front of them), then beheaded and the body chopped into four parts. Finally, the head was stuck on a pole and displayed as a warning to others.

King James decreed that henceforth people should celebrate deliverance from the conspiracy by lighting a bonfire each year on the date of Guy Fawkes' treachery. So across Britain in gardens, parks, fields and wasteland fire mania takes hold. And nowhere more dramatically than in Lewes, East Sussex and Bridgewater, Devon: both towns were staunchly Protestant at the time of the treason plot.

Guy Fawkes' Confession

If he will not other wayes confesse the gentler tortours are to be first used unto him, et sic per gradus ad mia tenditur [and so by degrees proceeding to the worst], and so God speed your goode worke.

James I gave those written instructions to guards at the Tower of London to authorise the torture of Guy Fawkes. Proof of the devastating effect such punishment had on his body is in the signature on his confession of 7 November – it is the shadow of a scrawl. He signed another confession eight days after the torture and that one is written in a steady hand. Both can be seen on the original documents in the National Archive collection.

In Lewes, Bonfire Night is one of the biggest dates in the calendar and the culmination of weeks of work by six societies that comprise Lewes Bonfire Council. These groups join together for a procession through town to the individual sites of their own conflagrations. They wear spectacular themed costumes, dressed for instance as cavaliers, Zulu warriors or Siamese dancers. Traditionally some members in each group disguise themselves as smugglers and carry flaming torches – some in the shape of crosses – at the head of the parade. These individuals either wear masks or black their faces with burnt cork. Each society carries an effigy of Guy Fawkes and sometimes a representation of Camillo Borghese, Pope at the time of the Gunpowder Plot, to be burned on the bonfire. Other effigies depicting current public enemies or hate figures are stuffed with fireworks and incinerated. Fireworks were traditionally used in Britain to mark great occasions.

Blazing tar barrels are either dragged along the street or carried on long poles and ceremonially thrown from the bridge into the river. Lewes' big night is hardly silent night as hundreds of fireworks explode during the procession – particularly bangers, known locally as 'rookies' or rook-scarers. There is an element of danger and a hint of anarchy to this fire festival. Not surprisingly, such an exuberant carnival attracts thousands of visitors.

Another major commemoration takes place in Bridgewater on the nearest Friday to Bonfire Night. This street party is often billed as the world's largest festival of illumination. It consists of a procession of some 150 floats decorated by individual carnival clubs. The parade is led by a float that depicts the discovery of Guy Fawkes in the cellar of the Houses of Parliament. Other floats are much more flamboyant, each one an individual *tableau vivant* representing a theme – such as the Wrath of Neptune, or Thor, God of Thunder – illuminated by thousands of light bulbs. Months of effort by the clubs go into designing the spectacle. Seen from above the street resembles a river of light not least because of squibbing. Unique to Bridgewater, squibbing is the simultaneous firing of hundreds of giant fireworks called 'squibs' manufactured especially for the carnival. Up to 150 squibbers line the high street holding 2-metre long wooden poles to which squibs are attached. As the fireworks are ignited the poles are held aloft, creating a cascade of sparks.

One of the oldest fire festivals is Ottery St Mary Tar Barrels. Originally, lighted tar barrels were rolled in the streets to celebrate 5 November but that was considered too tame and now the ultimate Bonfire Night ritual is exercised. People vie for the opportunity to run through the village carrying on their shoulders large barrels lined with coal tar and filled with straw and paper. Harmless? Hardly, the barrels are open at one end and the stuffing is soaked in paraffin then ignited so the carrier has an inferno on their back. Apart from wearing the sackcloth equivalent of oven gloves, the person hauling the barrel has no protection from the flames. Seventeen barrels are burned in total and there is much competition from all sexes and ages to carry them. Barrels are set alight outside the pub and the first carrier picks it up and runs down the street. The barrel passes from one person to another in relay until it falls to pieces and is dumped. High drama prevails as spectators scarper to avoid being scorched when the barrel brushes close by them in the narrow streets. But that's all part of the tradition.

Fire Festivals in Scotland

Fire festivals are not confined to Scotland but the Scots do them best, especially at Hogmanay. Celtic pagans believed that fire rituals would ward off evil spirits and protect them from disaster. Spirits are welcomed nowadays – as long as they come in a bottle. Latter-day fire festivals are celebrations and that usually means a nip or two of Scotland's national drink.

The Fireballs in Stonehaven, Aberdeenshire

Nobody welcomes in the New Year like the Scots. Hogmanay in Stonehaven near Aberdeen is a heated affair with a party known as The Fireballs – a festivity in which fireballs are swung through the air. Prior to midnight, puppeteers, dancers and musicians entertain in the high street but as the clock bell strikes midnight the fireballs start and the night is suddenly illuminated. Up to fifty locals take on the role of 'swinger', each enthusiastically swinging a fireball above their head. Imagine the effect when a sparkler is waved around: that's what fireballs resemble but immeasurably more spectacular. Fireballs weigh about 7 kilograms and comprise a chicken wire frame stuffed with combustibles such as newspaper, old rags, twigs, and pinecones, all doused with flammable liquid. The procession of swingers parades through the town, sparks flying, and ends up at the harbour into which the fireballs are hurled. But the merrymaking doesn't end there – a firework display lights up the sky and back in the town square fire jugglers deftly avoid burning their hands well into the night. Swinging the Fireballs was already a Stonehaven tradition in the 1880s but its provenance is unknown. Processions with flaming torches were common all over Europe up to the Middle Ages. There are two theories that may explain early fire festivals. One is purification – fire cleanses malevolent forces; the other is that fire mimics the sun during dark winter days.

Flambeaux Procession in Comrie, Perthshire

Another Hogmanay tradition is Comrie's atmospheric Flambeaux Procession. Flambeaux (the French word for torches) are saplings wrapped in hessian bags and soaked in paraffin. At midnight eight flambeaux (some more than 2 metres high) are kindled and carried on poles at the head of a procession of bagpipers and people in fancy dress. The parade meanders around the village, eventually reaching Dalginross Bridge where the flambeaux are thrown ceremoniously into the river. The origin of the Flambeaux Procession is unclear. Perhaps it is a revival of an older tradition where fire was used to ward off evil spirits.

FESTIVALS AND PAGEANTS

The Burning of the Clavie in Burghead, Morayshire

People who cannot wait a whole year between Hogmanay celebrations are in luck on 11 January. That day is called Old Yule Night, or Old Hogmanay, and is celebrated in the fishing village of Burghead. A clavie is a wooden half-barrel lined with tar and filled with sticks and wood shavings. The barrel is ritually nailed to a carrying post using the same nail year after year. When the practice began the container would have been a herring barrel but now a whisky cask is used. The contents are ignited and the Clavie King and his ten Clavie Crew take turns to carry the fireball through each street in the village. None of the crew wants to commit a faux pas by dropping the fiery cargo – that would be a bad omen for Burghead and the local fishing industry. Being a member of the Clavie Crew is a great honour passed down through generations of Burgheadians.

Hundreds of people follow the parade with spectators scrambling to pick up embers that fall from the clavie. These are much in demand as they bring good luck and are used to stoke a special New Year's fire that prevents evil spirits from coming down the chimney. Finally, the clavie is carried up to the top of Doorie Hill, former site of a Pictish fort, where it is mounted on a stone cairn and illuminates the night so dramatically it appears as though the hillside is on fire.

Perhaps not surprisingly, clavie burning was considered idolatrous by the dour leaders of the Presbyterian church in previous centuries – they considered such heathen practices sinful. But if something is fun it can't be suppressed and so the Clavie Crew continue their combustible tradition.

Up-Helly-Aa Festival in Lerwick, Shetland Islands

Fire, feasting and fancy dress is the recipe for Shetland's Up-Helly-Aa Festival, with plenty of spirit to add spice and unpredictability. If your dream is to encounter a Viking then visit Lerwick on the final Tuesday in January because the town is awash with them. Or at least, big hairy Shetlanders carrying shields and axes and dressed in raven-winged helmets, knee-skimming tunics and metal breastplates. The Shetland Isles' Norse heritage is celebrated in spectacular fashion with a fire festival that takes months of planning and is celebrated so enthusiastically that it can take months to recover from. At the centre of Up-Helly-Aa is an authentic wooden Viking long ship, complete with dragonhead prow, meticulously built by volunteers in the weeks preceding the festival.

On the night of the event the streets are lined with hundreds of guisers (torchbearers) all in costume, holding wooden fence posts topped with paraffin soaked sackcloth. A rocket that explodes over the town hall is the cue to ignite the torches and simultaneously a kilometre long river of fire erupts into flame. The principal character, Guiser Jarl, stands at the helm of the long ship as a squad of burly Vikings drags it through the town. The guisers are members of various squads each with its own theme and dressed accordingly. Later on they visit various parties and perform skits and dances based on their chosen subject. But for the moment they light up the night as the procession snakes along behind the boat.

All those hours of painstaking work are about to come to an end as the guisers surround the long ship in a circle of fire. Another rocket explodes and Guiser Jarl disembarks as a bugle made of animal horn sounds the signal for the guisers to hurl their torches onboard. As they do so they sing a requiem song, 'The Norseman's Home', an echo of the ritual of cremating a deceased Viking with his longboat.

Now the shindig really kicks off and continues until morning, fuelled by whisky and mutton soup. Guisers are expected to visit every party to dance with the women and drink to everyone's health.

To the uninformed, Lerwick resembles a ghost town the following day. It is a public holiday and the streets are quiet as everyone slumbers and recuperates from the pagan revelry. But these Vikings are made of strong stuff and that evening 'Hop Night' takes place, when more dancing and celebrations rock the rafters.

The Lost Days

If changing the clocks each year in March for an extra hour of daylight is confusing then spare a thought for the citizens of Scotland in 1600. King James VI introduced the Gregorian calendar to replace the Julian calendar because it more accurately matched the solar year. The trouble was, it meant losing eleven days at a stroke; all very well for prisoners counting down to release date, but there were cases of unscrupulous employers refusing to honour the wages of day labourers, and many people thought that their lives had been shortened by almost two weeks. England delayed before changing to the new calendar – waiting almost 152 years until 1752 when an Act of Parliament made the Gregorian system law. Until then people often used both Julian and Gregorian dates, which confused everybody. As early as the 1580s English intellectuals had urged the government to embrace the new calendar. It just took them a while to come to an agreement.

In Bloom

May Day Festivals, countrywide

Banish winter and welcome spring. After Christmas and New Year, May Day is the biggest reason for a party across Britain. Cold, miserable weather will soon be a memory replaced by the promise of blue skies. That alone deserves celebration. All over the country a diverse range of events mark this special day as maypoles, morris dancing, village fetes, May queens and flower garlands abound.

Maypoles on the village green were once common all over England and Wales when young men and women danced around the phallic symbol to promote their own sexual fertility, having fun flirting as they intertwined the hanging foliage. The origins of maypoles are in tree-spirit worship and in a Roman spring festival called *Floralia* held in honour of Flora the goddess of flowers. But seventeenth-century Puritans led by Oliver Cromwell disapproved of such un-Christian jollifications and proscribed maypole dancing as 'a heathenish vanity'. Cromwell attempted, with some success, to prohibit any entertainments where people had fun. Theatres were forcibly closed, alehouses suppressed, some sports banned. Religious worship was celebrated whilst pointless enjoyment was frowned upon. No wonder the maypoles had to go. But come the restoration of Charles II people relished the opportunity to dance without censure and once again maypoles were the joyful focus of May Day celebrations.

Maypoles are normally tall, striped and decorated with garlands and flags. Dancers hold on to ribbons that hang from the top of the pole and skip in interweaving steps to a folk music accompaniment until the ribbons are plaited. Today only a few towns and villages have a permanent maypole but that is no reason not to enjoy a dance – portable maypoles can be rented for the day. Which means that the sight of children and adults dancing the spider's web or the double plait to rejoice in the coming of spring is increasingly common.

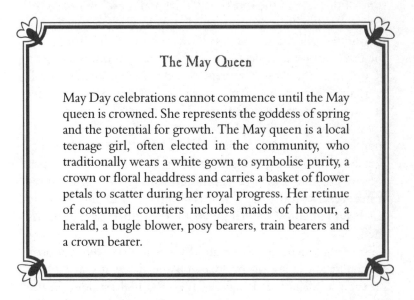

The May Queen

May Day celebrations cannot commence until the May queen is crowned. She represents the goddess of spring and the potential for growth. The May queen is a local teenage girl, often elected in the community, who traditionally wears a white gown to symbolise purity, a crown or floral headdress and carries a basket of flower petals to scatter during her royal progress. Her retinue of costumed courtiers includes maids of honour, a herald, a bugle blower, posy bearers, train bearers and a crown bearer.

Hundreds of towns and villages stage May Day fairs. A typical festival will incorporate maypole dancing, a fancy dress parade, a brass band, face painting, a tombola, pony rides, craft stalls and more. A number of fairs have unique elements. During the Royal May Day at Knutsford in Cheshire, pavements are sprinkled with coloured sand marked out with mottoes and patterns in a custom called 'sanding'. One of the oldest fairs is in Hereford and dates to 1117 when the bishop granted the privilege. Today, in lieu of rent for the church land on which the three-day extravaganza takes place, the bishop is ceremoniously presented with twelve and a half bushels of wheat.

Imagine May Day without a troupe of morris dancers jigging about in flower-trimmed costumes, waving white hankies in the air and ritually slapping sticks together to the rhythm of lively melodeon music. May Day is the busiest time of the year in the morris calendar and there are dozens of troupes throughout the country that welcome summer in the traditional folk dance manner. However, not every troupe has the opportunity to collect the May dew from around the head of a giant as the Wessex morris men do. Each year they climb up to the Cerne Abbas giant – a priapic figure cut into the chalk hillside – and dance at sunrise. Then they descend into the town and progress through the streets, dancing as they go. One member of the group carries the head of a fearsome looking, horned half-human wooden creature known as the Dorset Ooser. This beast may be connected with fertility worship or it may represent the devil. If it is an image of Lucifer then he has been tamed by the happy-go-lucky attitude of the morris men.

For King's Lynn May Garland Procession the king's morris men herald the spring by 'dancing the dawn up' at sunrise on the roundabout at Knight's Hill – the highest point in the borough. Later on they parade through the town carrying the May garland – a hoop decorated with flowers, greenery and ribbons that surrounds a doll mounted on a pole.

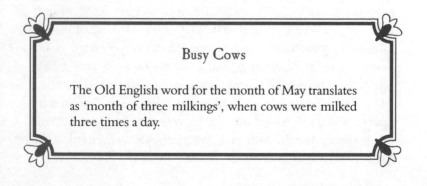

Busy Cows

The Old English word for the month of May translates as 'month of three milkings', when cows were milked three times a day.

Jack-in-the-Green in Hastings, East Sussex

Hastings has had its battles – most notably when those unsolicited Normans came knocking. Now on May Day Monday the only tussle is the one to be first to welcome Jack-in-the-Green as he is released from his sanctuary to greet the spring season. Jack may resemble a walking rhododendron bush but he is really a human being disguised under a 2-metre tall frame covered in green leaves, trimmed with coloured ribbons and topped by a charming floral crown that deserves to be stored in the Tower of London. He has a retinue of several hundred supporters including his attendants, the all-green bogie men, decked out in foliage, flowers, camouflage face paint, hair and beards died green and interwoven with leaves. They resemble a battalion of hirsute triffids. The exuberant atmosphere is enhanced by a number of costumed morris troupes, who dance everywhere they go. Children are pulled along the route in carts that appear to be mobile shrubbery, flower fairies dart about, women promenade in faux medieval gowns straight out of *Robin Hood* and groups of drummers beat a hypnotic rhythm.

When the procession reaches its destination on a cliff top where William of Normandy's castle once dominated the town it is time for an afternoon of dancing and jollity. However, not everyone will enjoy the proceedings. Someone is to be sacrificed for the benefit of the majority: poor Jack-in-the-Green. The bogie men accompany their friend Jack onto the stage where he is symbolically slain, his crown pulled off and foliage thrown to the crowd and retained for good luck. Jack's death releases the Spirit of Summer to bring happiness and good weather to all.

Jack-in-the-Green is an urban phenomenon largely confined to South East England. Jack is a non-dancing member of certain morris troupes in Whitstable, Rochester and Deptford.

Further afield in Bristol, May Day is celebrated with a 3-metre tall Jack. He progresses from the harbour up through the city to Horfield Common where he ritually dies to ensure the arrival of summer.

Jack-in-the-Chimney

May Day was traditionally a day off for workers. Beginning in the eighteenth century, it became a tradition for young men and women to show off elaborate home-made garlands and earn tips. Milkmaids in London wore intricate floral displays on their heads from which they hung the utensils of their trade – pots and silver cups – but it was the chimney sweeps that outdid everyone. They fashioned garlands that covered their entire bodies and went about collecting money for their efforts. This seasonal figure became known as Jack-in-the-Green. May Day was always a revel but the stern Victorians, who disapproved of the drunken behaviour, deemed Jack to be an excuse for begging and banned him. He reappeared in the 1960s when some folk customs were revived.

Garland Day in Castleton, Derbyshire

Castleton celebrates 29 May each year in delightful fashion with Garland Day when two villagers nominated as the king and queen parade on horseback. Both characters wear seventeenth-century velvet costumes decorated with lace, ribbons and ostrich feathers. Just as the peacock is endowed with a more splendid plumage than the peahen, so the king's get-up attracts all eyes. In addition to his Stuart era attire he wears the garland – a 1-metre high beehive-shaped frame on which bunches of wild flowers and leaves are attached. The king requires stamina because it weighs over 25 kilograms and obscures the top half of his body.

A small wreath of garden flowers crowns the garland – this is called the 'queen', not to be confused with Her Majesty on the horse. A merry procession comprised of a brass band, female morris dancing troupe and plenty of spectators follow the floral vision. Everyone stops outside the village pubs, six in total, where the troupe dances and people have a drink before assembling at the Maypole for more jollity. Then the liberation of the king takes place. The garland is lifted from his shoulders, tied to a rope and hoisted up the steeple of St Edmund's parish church where it is left to wither away. The queen posy is ceremonially placed on the war memorial in the village square. Then everyone continues singing, dancing and drinking into the evening.

This is a hybrid event that combines a May Garland Day and Oak Apple Day. The latter dates from 1660 when the Stuart King Charles II was restored to the throne after the death of Lord Protector Oliver Cromwell. Charles was a party boy and one of his first declarations was for an annual public holiday on his birthday, 29 May. That date also marks the day Charles returned from exile to London. With a new excuse for a revel, trees were decorated with flags and flowers and people caroused and toasted the restoration of the king. Oak apple refers to the oak tree in which Charles took cover during the Civil War as he escaped from enemy soldiers. That mythical tree inspired one of Britain's most popular pub names – the Royal Oak.

Castleton's Blue John

If the value of minerals were assessed by the number of mines that extract them then diamonds and emeralds would be worthless and Blue John priceless. Blue John is found at only one location in the world – Treak Cliff Hill just outside Castleton in the heart of Derbyshire's Peak District National Park. The name is a corruption of the French – *bleu jaune* (blue yellow). The mineral is a distinctive banded blue/purple and yellow fluorite used as a gemstone in costume jewellery, bowls and goblets and gives Castleton its nickname – 'gem of the peaks'.

Well Dressing, in the Peak District, Derbyshire and Staffordshire

Nature and artistry unite in spectacular style for the annual well dressing season. In a charming custom that has echoes of pre-Christian water worship, springs and public wells are exquisitely decorated with works of art that resemble paintings. But rather than being created with paint on canvas, the images are crafted by attaching local plant life to a wooden board. Religious themes are popular, so are commemorations of national anniversaries, and even issues that concern residents such as the campaign to save rural post offices. When it comes to well dressing the imagination knows no bounds.

This glorious salutation of water happens at dozens of sites, primarily in the Peak District of Derbyshire and Staffordshire. Dressing a well is a community activity that involves everyone – adult and child. Once a decision has been made about design, the materials for creating it can be gathered. This is where children comb the countryside collecting the vegetation necessary to make an elaborate floral picture. Depending on the season this might include blossoms, flower petals, seeds, leaves, twigs, bark, moss and berries.

Before the wooden boards can be decorated they must be soaked for a few days in the pond or a stream. This is crucial because damp clay is smeared over the board and then the plant-life is pressed into it. If the boards were not impregnated with water the wood would suck moisture from the clay and it would quickly dry out causing the artwork to collapse. To prepare the clay, volunteers undertake a task known as puddling. Wearing wellies, they stand in an old tank or tin bath and tread through the glutinous muck to ensure that water is mixed through it.

Now the artistic endeavour can begin. A thick layer of clay is daubed on the wooden base and a design etched into the soft surface. Constructing the elaborate tableau is painstaking work as thousands of appropriately coloured petals, seeds and berries are attached. This is not a task that can be hurried – it may require ten days (and nights) of non-stop work, but all the effort is forgotten in the thrill of seeing the masterpiece completed. With great ceremony the dressing is erected adjacent to the well and blessed by a vicar. If a town has more than one well each of them will be dressed and blessed.

Tissington is a model English estate village that boasts a duck pond, tearooms, a Norman church and Jacobean manor house. Although the origin of well dressing is unclear, villagers believe that the ritual dates back at least to 1348 when the Black Death decimated countless communities. Tissington escaped the plague and the locals attributed that to the purity of the water. In thanksgiving they dressed the wells with flowers. The custom lapsed but was revived in 1615 as grateful thanks for the water that kept flowing during a severe drought. Nowadays Tissington's well-dressing festival is one of the earliest – it starts on Ascension Day with a procession around the village's six wells.

Between May and September, locals and visitors delight in the creativity of the well-dressing artists. Over the summer period it is possible to tour towns and villages in the Peak District and see the latest well dressing. But hurry – this is art at its most ephemeral because only a week or so after the well is dressed the decoration starts to fall off and the dressing is retired, until next year when a new creation will take its place.

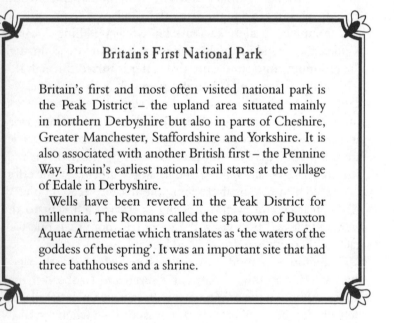

Britain's First National Park

Britain's first and most often visited national park is the Peak District – the upland area situated mainly in northern Derbyshire but also in parts of Cheshire, Greater Manchester, Staffordshire and Yorkshire. It is also associated with another British first – the Pennine Way. Britain's earliest national trail starts at the village of Edale in Derbyshire.

Wells have been revered in the Peak District for millennia. The Romans called the spa town of Buxton Aquae Arnemetiae which translates as 'the waters of the goddess of the spring'. It was an important site that had three bathhouses and a shrine.

Dance Fever

Coco-Nut Dancing in Bacup, Lancashire

Unique is an overused word, but in the case of Britannia Coco-Nut Dancers it is accurate. Of the hundreds of folk dance troupes in Britain none resembles Bacup's finest musical export. For a start, each dancer in the eight-man troupe wears a white, thigh-skimming, kilt-like skirt hemmed with red and white horizontal stripes. This is contrasted with a black long-sleeved sweatshirt and white over-the-shoulder sash, and black knee breeches worn with white socks and black clogs. On their heads the men wear a white turban trimmed with a blue feather, red pom-pom and a rosette. The look is completed with blackened faces. This might originally have been a disguise to avoid being recognised by evil spirits, although in the case of Bacup it could be related to the appearance of miners in the local coal industry.

On their hands, knees and belt the dancers sport maple wood discs or 'coconuts' that are struck together in time to the music to form a distinctive clip-clop sound. One dancer holds a whip – he is the 'whiffler' or 'whipper in' – and leads the troupe and cracks the whip to drive away bad spirits. Each man carries an arched floral garland for ritual dances associated with the renewal of crops in spring.

The Nutters, as they call themselves, are invited to perform at festivals and special events around the country and they always dance in their hometown on Easter Saturday. On that special day the musical accompaniment is a brass band – any other time it is a concertina.

Why would such an exotic dance troupe originate in industrial east Lancashire? One theory is that Moorish sailors settled in

Cornwall and brought their dances (and dress sense) with them. When Lancashire's coal mining industry expanded in the eighteenth century, Cornish miners moved north looking for work and imported some of their cultural practices. By the turn of the nineteenth century there were four such troupes but now the Nutters are the only exponents of the inimitable style of coco-nut dancing.

Muddy Valley by a Ridge

Bacup is called 'Fulebachope' in a charter written in 1200. The *Oxford Dictionary of British Place Names* translates it as 'muddy valley by a ridge'. Seven hundred years later Bacup was a productive cotton-weaving mill town. Claims that the 5-metre long Elgin Street is the shortest street in the world have not been verified.

Flora Day in Helston, Cornwall

For most people 'Dancing in the Street' is the name of a well-known pop tune but to the residents of Helston it refers to Flora Day. That is when the town transforms into an open-air dance hall as thousands of Helstonians and visitors meander through the streets in a mass processional couples' dance. They do not just keep to the thoroughfares, though, because the dance has a mind of its own and may also lead into gardens, houses, shops, inns and other public buildings. It can take an hour to complete so this is more like a marathon than a sprint. To help keep the dancers' rhythm Helston Town Band plays a tune called 'The Flora Dance'.

It normally happens on 8 May when the blossom is glorious and the town looks its best decked with colourful flags and locally picked foliage – bluebells, laurel leaves and gorse. Many townsfolk wear Sunday best, especially the ones who plan to dance. Traditionally, dancers wear a buttonhole of Lily of the Valley – Helston's symbolic flower.

Festivities start at 7 a.m. with the first of four dances that take place throughout the day. The early dance was originally reserved for the servant class but now it is open to any adult providing the men wear shirt and tie and the ladies are in light summer dresses. After the gentle musical alarm call it is time for something completely different. Costumed characters gather to perform a boisterous pageant known as 'Hal-an-Tow'. The main characters represent St George slaying the dragon and St Michael triumphing over Lucifer, and the ritual is repeated at a number of locations in town as the battle of good versus evil is fought and won.

At 10 a.m. it is the turn of children from local schools. They form a procession up to 1,000 strong in which everyone is dressed in white. The boys wear a school tie and the girls' hair is trimmed with flowers that correspond to their school colour – forget-me-nots, daisies, poppies or cornflowers.

The main or 'principal dance' begins at midday outside the Corn Exchange, with the place resembling a scene from *My Fair Lady* – men in top hats and morning coats, women smartly attired in long gowns and wide-brimmed picture hats. Hand in hand with their partners they form a dignified parade through the narrow streets. Participation in this dance is by invitation only and it is a great honour to be included. At 5 p.m. the final dance takes place with the performers expected to wear shirt and tie and summer frocks.

Flora Day is also known as Furry Day and some locals suggest that it originated as a pagan spring festival. According to written records of the time it was certainly well established in the late eighteenth century. In those days Flora Day was a highly spirited affair, so much so that elements of it were suppressed in the nineteenth century because of drunken shenanigans that might then have been described by polite society as barbarous. Nowadays, Flora Day has a carnival atmosphere but few troublemakers in the thousands of visitors that throng the streets and pubs well into the night.

Coinagehall Street

Helston's connection with Cornwall's historic tin mining industry is apparent in the name of the town's main thoroughfare, Coinagehall Street. During the thirteenth century, in the reign of Edward I, Helston became a coinage town where miners assembled to have their tin weighed and assayed.

Horn Dance in Abbots Bromley, Staffordshire

Where did six sets of reindeer antlers that have hung for centuries on the wall in St Nicholas parish church come from? Carbon testing of one set suggests they date from 1065, and at that time there were no reindeer in Britain. Were they imported from Scandinavia and if so, why? It is not known when the horns first arrived in Abbots Bromley but as long as anyone can remember they have been put to good use on Wakes Monday (old St Bartholomew's Day in early September) when they become the focal point of the one-of-a-kind Horn Dance.

Twelve characters in costume perform the Horn Dance. The principals are six Deer Men who carry the antlers so they extend upwards from the chest to give the impression they are attached to the body – half man, half reindeer: a reinman. The antlers are actually mounted on a short pole attached to a small, carved wooden deer head so they are held rather than worn. Other group members are the jester, Maid Marian (a man in drag), a man riding a hobby horse, a melodeon player and two youths – one carrying a bow and arrow, the other keeping the beat by clanging a triangle.

The dancing day begins at 8 a.m. with a blessing from the vicar as the troupe collects the antlers from the church. They spend the next twelve hours performing the dance outside pubs, farms and at local landmarks during a 16-kilometre journey around the village. In total the dancers perform their routine twelve times in as many locations. Dressed in pantomime-style medieval outfits of jerkin, knee breeches, knitted stockings and a cap – designed in the 1850s by the vicar's wife – they are an eye-catching sight.

Horn dancing is a highlight in the village year and dancers are warmly welcomed. The dance starts off with little fanfare as the horn men stand in a silent circle. When the music begins they form two opposite lines and in deliberate and rhythmical steps advance towards and then retreat from their counterpart tilting the horns but not aggressively locking them. All the while the hobby horse man snaps the jaws of his equine costume as the triangle keeps the beat and Maid Marian and the jester entertain on the sidelines. Strictly Come Horn Dancing is not for wimps because each set of antlers spans between 75 centimetres and 1 metre and weighs more than 7 kilograms, the heaviest being over 11 kilograms. Those reindeer must have been the alpha males of their herds.

Since the early twentieth century members of the same clan have comprised the dance troupe. They were related to the family who kept the tradition alive until the end of the nineteenth century. No one knows when the dance was first performed. Some reports suggest that it was in 1226 at the St

Bartholomew's Day (Barthelmy) Fair. The earliest written reference appears in the *Natural History of Staffordshire* (1686), where the author Robert Plot makes reference to both the hobby horse and reindeer antlers.

Another mystery is the original purpose. There are several suggestions. It may originally have been a ceremony to ensure bountiful hunting and to celebrate common land rights in the Forest of Needwood. Or perhaps it was a fertility ritual. Could there be a connection with the rutting season, when male deer challenge each other by locking antlers together?

The Horn Dance is a magnet for visitors who flock to the village to experience a unique event. Its reputation reaches far and the dancers accept regular invitations to stage it elsewhere. But the precious reindeer antlers do not go with them. When the dancers travel they take substitute red deer horns because the priceless originals never leave Abbots Bromley parish boundaries. Those impressive crowns are on display in their sacred home waiting for that one special day when they are given their annual outing.

Forest of Needwood

Abbots Bromley is situated within the ancient Forest of Needwood, a vast property that was bestowed on Edmund, First Earl of Lancaster, in 1266. The current lord of the manor is the Duke of Lancaster, also surprisingly known as Elizabeth II. Duke of Lancaster is one of the monarch's titles, but not Duchess of Lancaster. Queen Victoria considered 'duke' to be a proper title for the holder of a dukedom, whether man or woman, whereas 'duchess' was a courtesy title for a duke's consort.

Morris Dancing, countrywide

Follow the sound of a concertina at a May fair or outside a pub on Boxing Day for it will invariably lead to a troupe of morris men performing traditional folk dances. Those symbols of Merrie England are a reminder of a bucolic past before the Industrial Revolution begat those 'dark satanic mills' and the majority of Britons moved away from the countryside to live in towns and cities.

Morris dancing is all about fun and for anyone who likes a jig and to dress up in costume this is the ideal pastime. Each morris troupe has its own attire depending on which style of dancing it specialises in. The classic costume includes white shirts, breeches, socks and black shoes, baldrics – ornamental sashes worn over the shoulder and tied at the hip – hats decorated with feathers, flowers, badges or all three, ribbons, rosettes and sleigh bells on pads attached to the shin. In addition to the main dancers there are a number of characters on the periphery – an extravagantly dressed fool who sometimes carries an inflated bladder on the end of a stick and interacts with the audience through speech or mime, a hobby – commonly a horse's head with a dancer underneath it – and a bagman who holds his hat out to collect cash donations from the crowd. After all, the troupe will require liquid refreshment later.

There are several traditions of morris dancing. These were formerly confined to the regions they originated in but morris troupes today choose which style they want to follow and are not dictated to by geography. They are:

Cotswold: This is the most widely practised technique. Dancers wave handkerchiefs in the air or clash wooden sticks together.

Border (from the English–Welsh border counties): A boisterous style using wooden sticks. Dancers normally blacken their faces. This custom originated as a disguise and has no racist connotations. These dancers do not resemble the classic image of a morris dancer because they wear black tattered suits with white shirts onto which coloured rags are sewn. Black flat caps or bowlers are worn.

North-west: Dancers wear clogs with bells attached to them and twirl twisted cotton rope, called mollies or slings, or wave painted sticks adorned with bells and ribbons. The processional dances are normally performed with at least eight dancers arranged in two files. Unlike other morris traditions, North-west has included female dancers since at least the early nineteenth century.

Molly: This version of morris dancing is now largely confined to a few troupes in East Anglia. It is a pared down variety where bells, wooden sticks and traditional costume motifs are sacrificed in favour of face painting and a chance to wear women's clothes. Originally, agricultural workers danced to earn money in the winter season when farm work was scarce. Those people who refused to hand over any coins would be penalised, for instance by having a furrow ploughed across their garden. To protect identities the dancers blackened their faces. One of the group wears a dress – he is the Molly.

Two other folk dances are sometimes classified with morris, although their exponents do not always consider themselves to be part of that tradition. Longsword dancing is traditional in Yorkshire and Cleveland, whilst in Northumberland and

County Durham rapper or short sword dancing is practised. These dance styles exhibit a military influence and the dancers wear sober costumes that resemble uniforms. No blacked out faces, bells or garlands there.

Longsword dancing requires five to eight performers to carry a rigid metal bars or wooden panels that measure about 1 metre. The dance starts with rhythmic clashing of the 'swords' as the dancers form a ring, each person holding the point of his neighbour's sword. As the routine progresses in a collection of weaving and twisting movements the aim is to plait the swords together and hold them aloft.

In a rapper dance a five-strong troupe is connected with short two-handled flexible swords (rappers) to form a chain. Dancers weave in and out of each other forming prescribed shapes with the rappers, sometimes even jumping or somersaulting over the swords. The dance also includes two comedy characters – Tommy and Betty. Tommy provides an amusing commentary on the proceedings and interacts with Betty – a large man, usually bearded, who wears a dress.

A folk dance revival in the 1960s prompted the resurgence of morris dancing and there are now several hundred sides in Britain. One of them, the Abingdon Morris Dancers in Oxfordshire, claims an unbroken tradition that dates to at least 1700. The highlight of their performing year is in mid-June with the election of the mayor of Ock Street, a thoroughfare in Abingdon. This is a mock ceremony when residents of the street choose a 'mayor'. They can vote for whom they like as long as he is the squire (leader) of the morris troupe. As soon as the election result is declared the new mayor with his regalia of sword, mace, and applewood and silver chalice is carried aloft through his constituency in a chair decorated with flower garlands. Visiting morris troupes come to pay homage and they all participate in a cheerful celebratory feast that lasts until midnight.

Abingdon Morris Dancers have a repertoire of fifteen dances with names such as 'Princes Royal', 'Gentleman Jack', 'Curly Headed Ploughboy', 'The Girl I left Behind Me', 'Buttercup Joe', 'Jockeys to The Fair', and 'How d'ye Do Sir'. The side never performs without the antique Ock Street horns – a carved wood oxen mask with real animal horns on a long pole garlanded with flowers.

If just one image had to encapsulate British traditions, surely a photo of a troupe of morris dancers in action must be a contender.

Moorish Origins?

The word morris is believed to be a derivation of *mouresca, moresque* or *morisco*, European terms for 'Moorish', because it was a style of dance that the Moors of North Africa supposedly practised. The earliest reference to English morris dancing is 1448 in London. During the reign of Elizabeth I, morris dancing was already widely established and so much part of the culture that in many contemporary plays the lead actor would be required to do a little jig. Morris dancing waned in the eighteenth century due to social changes wrought by the Industrial Revolution and its practice declined further in the nineteenth century.

Music to the Ears

Horn Blowing in Bainbridge and Ripon, Yorkshire

North Yorkshire could be forgiven for blowing its own horn. It is considered by many to be one of the most beautiful parts of the country. As well as doing it figuratively the county has two traditions where horns really are blown – one in Bainbridge and the other in Ripon.

Bainbridge is a remote Yorkshire Dales village formerly surrounded by the vast Forest of Wensleydale. Each night at 10 p.m. from the end of September to Shrove Tuesday a hunting horn is blown outside the pub. The horn hangs in the Rose & Crown Hotel and for generations the same local family has had the honour of sounding it. No one knows when or why the custom began. One theory is that it was a curfew warning, another that it was a signal to guide anyone lost in the dense forest to safety in the village.

In addition to the horn, Bainbridge is known for England's shortest river, the Bain. The waterway runs for only 3 kilometres from Semer Water to the River Ure. Semer, or Simmer Water means 'the lake pool' in Old English and it has an associated legend.

A weary traveller arrived in the village of Simmerdale and went from house to house begging for food and shelter. Despite being an affluent settlement everyone refused to help the beggar except one poor widow who offered a mug of ale. The traveller was so shocked at the lack of hospitality from other villagers that he cursed them saying: 'Simmerdale, Simmerdale, Simmerdale sink. Save the house of the woman who gave me a drink.' Then the valley magically filled with water and the village was drowned. Only the generous widow's cottage was saved.

Ripon has only 16,000 residents but it is classified as a city (albeit one of England's smallest) by virtue of its twelfth-century cathedral. The wakeman's horn ritual is a popular tourist attraction. Each night at 9 p.m. the wakeman proceeds to Market Place resplendent in a tricorn hat and eighteenth-century frock coat. To signal the start of the (former) night-time watch he stands by the obelisk and blasts his cow horn three times on each of the four sides, then again outside the adjacent mayor's house. This custom is believed to date from the thirteenth century when the wakeman was responsible for overnight crime prevention.

Ripon has four horns – the oldest is the Charter Horn that hangs on a baldric (ornamental belt) studded with silver emblems in the town hall. It is centuries old, although the exact age is unknown. Two reserve horns date from 1690 and 1886. The day-to-day horn was acquired in 1865 and is ceremoniously carried in front of the mayor whenever he attends formal events at the cathedral. Ripon's first citizen is mindful of the ancient role of the wakeman because an image of a horn and a line from Psalm 127 is etched on the mayor's badge of office: 'Except the Lord keep the city the watchman waketh but in vain.'

The Wakeman's Insurance

Ripon's wakeman employed constables to patrol the streets and prevent crime. They had to be thorough because if anyone was burgled the wakeman was bound to compensate the victims. To minimise the potential hole in his pocket the town council authorised him to levy an annual tax on houses. The amount due depended on how many outside doors a dwelling had: four pence for two doors and tuppence for one door.

Whit Walks and Brass Bands Competitions in Saddleworth, Lancashire

Each year on Whit Friday Saddleworth becomes embouchure capital of the world. Embouchure is a word that describes the puckering of lips on the mouthpiece of a woodwind or brass musical instrument. Saddleworth earns the distinction because of the Whit Walks and Brass Band Competitions. That is when almost 150 brass bands each with up to twenty-five members, descend on a dozen or so remote moorland towns and villages between Yorkshire and Lancashire for the greatest free show in the Pennines. Music lovers flock to the area for what is surely the highlight of brass band musicianship. Since 1884 Saddleworth has welcomed bands from all over Britain and the world to participate in a great institution that marks the festival of Whitsuntide, fifty days after Easter Sunday.

Once a common sight throughout Britain, Whit Friday Walks are now largely confined to a corner of north-west England. Saddleworth wholeheartedly celebrates the tradition when parishioners participate in their village's 'Procession of Witness'. Church clergy, children carrying baskets of flowers, scouts and guide troops, choirs and local families march around the parish singing hymns. Villages that do not have a resident brass band to lead the procession are adopted for the morning by visiting bands. The players give their embouchures a good workout in anticipation of the musical marathon that takes place later that day.

Uniforms are brushed up, instruments polished and music scores assembled in preparation for the battle of the bands. For these recitals musicians require not only talent but stamina too, because it is likely they will perform in twenty or so separate locations during the competition. Organisation skills are priceless, as bands scramble to reach the next stop in their schedule on time. Picture the scene as some 150 coaches negotiate the area's rural byways, rushing from one village to another, never mind the crowds of spectators who temporarily increase the population of Saddleworth by a few thousand.

Border Country

Saddleworth is a remote largely uninhabited moorland landscape on the border of Yorkshire and Lancashire. Villages with memorable names such as Delph, Diggle, Dobcross and Grotton are scattered throughout the area. Saddleworth is an anomaly because although it is within the boundaries of Yorkshire, Oldham Council in Lancashire administers it. This is a thorn in the side of the Saddleworth White Rose Society. It organises events on Yorkshire Day (1 August) as a reminder that the area is geographically a part of the West Riding of Yorkshire.

Contests typically start at 4.30 p.m. and end some time after 10.30 p.m. Performances are all open-air and each band is required to present two pieces of music – one must be a published march played on the move, and the other is played standing still. Adjudicators listen 'blind' – hidden round the corner or inside a building, unable to see which band is playing so they cannot be accused of favouritism. Some of the world's leading brass bands take part including the Brighouse and Rastrick. But this is not just about superstars and so the local Dobcross Youth Band is judged on equal terms with the internationally renowned Black Dyke Band. Each town or village runs its own contest organised by local volunteers. Running costs and prize money are collected throughout the year in numerous fund-raising events. Bands can enter as many individual contests as they want and may end up being multiple champions.

Whit Friday is a feat of endurance not just for the competitors but also the judges and audience. It is not unusual for fifty bands to perform in the bigger contests and that means non-stop musical entertainment into the small hours.

As the final notes fade and everyone starts to make their way home a satisfied sigh whispers over the moors and Saddleworth settles down for the night. But it won't be long before plans are underway for the following Whitsuntide and another peerless showcase of the best of brass.

Sporting Life

Many of the most popular sports in the world were pioneered in Britain – rugby, golf, football (soccer). Our national teams may not always dominate when playing, say, against New Zealand at rugby, the USA at golf or anyone in football. But, as the following chapter proves, there are some highly entertaining and singular sports where Britons reign supreme.

Ball Games

Hailes at Edinburgh Academy, Edinburgh, Scotland

When it comes to playing the ball game of hailes, Edinburgh Academy has no competition. That's because hailes is unique to that particular school. A match is held at the end of each summer term as a send-off for the final year pupils. Players comprise teams of leavers and prefects, or ephors (an ancient Greek term that means 'one who oversees'). Team size depends on the number of prefects – usually around sixteen – matched with the same amount of leavers. With up to seventy leavers there are several teams – each one taking its turn to play against the ephors.

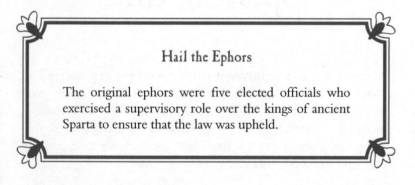

Hail the Ephors

The original ephors were five elected officials who exercised a supervisory role over the kings of ancient Sparta to ensure that the law was upheld.

The annual showdown takes place in the quadrangle and the entire school turns out to watch as the teams – boys and girls aged seventeen and eighteen – stroll out dressed in a variety of costumes, some armed with water pistols. Many boys choose to wear a frock, togas are always popular, and Roman centurions have made their mark.

Each player carries a clacken – a flat maple-wood paddle shaped like a spoon approximately 45 centimetres in length.

The name derives from *cleckinbrod* – from the Scots words *cleck* meaning noisy, and *brod*: a board. For as long as anyone can remember a local company has supplied the school with the specialist equipment. Leavers keep the clacken – traditionally signed by everyone involved in the event – as a memento of their final school days.

To start a match the referee throws a tennis ball up into the air and the players lunge to hit it towards their team's goal – or *hail* (a Scots term for goal). They score by whacking the ball against a specific area of wall at opposing ends of the quadrangle. Hailes could be described as a hybrid of lacrosse, tennis and hockey but with an implement that has a hitting surface not much larger than a fist. Handling or kicking the ball is not permitted, but dribbling and running whilst bouncing it on the clacken is. This game may sound easy but imagine how difficult an egg and spoon race would be if a mob of defenders tried to crack the egg each time the finishing line came into view. And players must avoid being bashed by a flailing clacken as eager attackers attempt a mid-air intercept. This is cut-throat. After ten noisy minutes each way with school pupils and teachers cheering from the perimeter and every window the game ends. The team with the winning score is awarded a brass clacken – this is symbolic because the trophy remains on school premises.

Edinburgh Academy was founded in 1824 and at that time variations of hailes were played across Scotland. Its popularity waned throughout the country but remained at the academy as part of the general sports schedule, slowly dying out until it was showcased only for the end-of-school-year celebration.

Cricket Match on the Brambles, The Solent

Even if the organisers wanted to play this annual late summer cricket match more often, they could not. That is because it takes place on the Brambles – a sandbank that emerges from the Solent for just under an hour once a year during the lowest spring tide. This phenomenon is highly anticipated by members of the Royal Southern Yacht Club at Hamble in Hampshire and the Island Sailing Club (Isle of Wight) because since 1984 they have fielded teams for the fleeting showdown.

The Brambles is situated between Calshot on the mainland and the Isle of Wight at Cowes. Tidal charts accurately predict when it will surface so dozens of boats packed with players and spectators anchor near the marker buoy waiting for the sea level to drop. As soon as the sandbank materialises everyone jumps off their craft and wades onto the sand. First things first – the Bramble Inn is installed with tables, chairs and an umbrella to serve drinks to onlookers. Then when the stumps are set and the scoreboard erected the umpire declares play in a narrow arena that measures no more than a few dozen metres in length.

Just as in any proper English cricket game players wear whites, although some are barefoot with their trouser legs rolled up. Whereas waterlogged pitches would normally prevent play, on the Brambles puddles cannot be avoided. Players splash about the narrow arena with fielding provided by enthusiastic children and dogs in the outfield. Scoring is inaccurate although that has no bearing on the result because the teams take it in turns to win. Then in what seems like only minutes play is abandoned as the waves creep back to reclaim the Brambles for the deep. People rush to dismantle the Bramble Inn and, carrying everything they brought with them barely forty-five minutes earlier, retreat to their boats and sail away until the following year.

Drowned Valley

The Solent is a stretch of sea that separates Hampshire and the Isle of Wight. It is the drowned valley of a river that was overwhelmed by meltwater after the Ice Age. Over thousands of years it has gradually widened and deepened. Now it is a sailing playground and one of Britain's busiest shipping lanes, with craft heading to and from the ports of Southampton and Portsmouth.

Mass Ball Games, countrywide

Rugby: a contact sport played by teams who consider bruises, bloody noses, cauliflower ears and gashed limbs as nothing more than the usual outcome of a Sunday afternoon friendly.

Imagine joining in a game and being the person holding the ball as a barrage of hefty blokes blocks out the light with one intention: to show no mercy. At least in rugby there are rules – in mass ball games anarchy reigns. Players do not bother with anything as effete as a sports pitch – no, the battle is fought through the streets. These games are exceedingly boisterous but rarely violent, although minor injuries are common. Local businesses sensibly shut up shop for the day making sure to barricade the windows, and car owners remember to park well away from the action – preferably in the neighbouring town.

Several places in England and Scotland stage an annual mass ball game, historically played to coincide with religious festivals or holidays. In the case of Kirkwall in the Orkney Islands there are two games: one on Christmas Eve and another on New Year's Eve; Workington in Cumbria at Easter; and in Atherstone in Warwickshire, Sedgefield in County Durham, Ashbourne in Derbyshire, and Columb St Major in Cornwall, the games are played at Shrovetide. These games have been contested for centuries, originally parish versus parish, or apprentices of one trade against another.

Regardless of where they are played the latter-day games have similarities: one is that dozens, sometimes hundreds of people join in, the other is the scrum. A scrum is a pile of wriggling bodies in which the ball is concealed. To the uninitiated it may look as though everyone is having a rest just quietly lying there sometimes for minutes until the impasse suddenly ends when someone extricates the ball and breaks free of the crowd. But not for long, as the mob storms after it eager for another body-hugging clinch. Where a player lives in town determines what team they join. Sides are commonly referred to as Uppies and Downies (or some similar local term).

At Ashbourne the demarcation of town is the river Henmore, those born to its north are the Up'ards and those south are the Down'ards. This game is played with a hand-painted leather ball filled with cork to ensure it floats when it lands in the river. Two games are played, one on Shrove Tuesday, the other on Ash Wednesday and they are marathons. They begin in the town centre at 2 p.m. and must be over by 10 p.m. The object is for players to throw the ball at one of two goalposts, these are old millstones 5 kilometres apart on the riverbank. Players can score only by standing in the water to aim.

Ashbourne's game has several rules. One of them, now lapsed, stated that players must not murder their opponents. This has been replaced by: 'Players must not intentionally cause harm to others.' Other regulations stipulate that the ball must not be hidden in bags or rucksacks, or be transported on motorised vehicles, and play must be kept out of churchyards, the cemetery and the Memorial Gardens. Otherwise, anything goes.

Jedburgh is situated at a strategic river crossing on the Scottish Borders. From the thirteenth to seventeenth century the border between England and Scotland was not clearly defined. It was turbulent and lawless land with violent 'reivers' (an old name for robbers or bandits) killing anyone who tried to stop them carrying out all too frequent raids to steal cattle and other valuables. During that period political relations between the two countries was strained and there was always some reason for English soldiers to march into Scotland and create havoc and vice versa. This toughened up the men of Jedburgh and made them adept at using the 'Jeddart staff', a long pole tipped with a metal hook. A local legend talks of the town's ball game, the hand ba', originating when victorious Jedburgh soldiers played with the decapitated head of a foolhardy English general after his troops were trounced in a bloody skirmish. Judging by the intensity of today's game that could well be true. Jeddart (also known as Jethart) Hand Ba' is normally played in early February with a straw-stuffed leather ball decorated with ribbons. Players from the Uppies and Doonies manhandle the ball up alleyways, in backyards, gardens and anywhere else the scrum surges with the intention of 'hailing' the ball to their side of town and winning the game.

Cornish hurling is a team sport of Celtic origin (no relation to Irish hurling) in which a silver ball the size of an orange is passed from player to player in a move called dealing. An unruly version of the game is played in Columb St Major, Cornwall, on Shrove Tuesday and the second on the following Saturday. Teams play with a locally crafted ball of applewood covered in silver leaf.

At the start of the match the traditional proclamation is made: 'Town and country do your best. But in this parish I must rest.' Then the ball is thrown into an expectant crowd of hundreds and a battle between the Townsmen and Countrymen commences. A combination of shoving, pulling and throwing moves the ball over one or the other's boundary line, each a kilometre outside town. The action is good-natured and often stops so the ball can be passed gently to a child or elderly person. The player who succeeds in scoring the goal is hoisted aloft the shoulders of his team-mates and is borne into town for the 'drinking the silver ball' ceremony. In the evening the ball is taken around the pubs and dipped into jugs of ale. That 'silver beer' is shared and anyone who drinks it will have good luck for the coming year.

Sometimes Fighting, Murder and a Great Loss of Blood

Philip Stubbes, a Puritan pamphleteer writing in his book *The Anatomie of Abuses* (1583), described the violence of ball games:

… sometimes their necks are broken, sometimes their backs, sometimes their legs, sometimes their arms, sometimes one part is thrust out of joint, sometimes the noses gush out with blood… Football encourages envy and hatred… sometimes fighting, murder and a great loss of blood.

Sport by Any Other Name

Bog Snorkelling World Championship in Llanwrtyd Wells, Powys, Wales

Arguably the world's dirtiest championship sport takes place each year in Britain's smallest town – Llanwrtyd Wells (population circa 600). That's where hundreds of contenders from around the globe gather each August to compete for the title World Champion Bog Snorkeller. The aim is to swim for two lengths of a 55-metre trench specially cut from the Waen Rhydd peat bog. That may sound easy but the rules prohibit any swimming strokes – competitors wear flippers and have to propel themselves by kicking and nothing else. Snorkels are essential for breathing because entrants may only lift their heads from underneath the murky water for orientation purposes. Wetsuits are advisable because the bog water is filthy and very cold and a streamlined suit may offer a split second advantage – something to be grabbed in the fierce competition of this sport.

The muddy aquanauts need all the encouragement the crowds of spectators can offer because the brackish water has a soupy consistency that makes the undertaking harder than it looks, particularly for those who compete in fancy dress.

If human momentum does not appeal there is another option – the World Mountain Bike Bog Snorkelling Championship. Equally dirty but with a different skill required: cycling. This is unlike any other bicycle sport. Bike frames are packed with lead and tyres filled with water to ensure that the cycle grips the bog. Competition is held in a 40-metre long water-filled trench that is 2 metres deep. Competitors wear a wetsuit, mask, snorkel and a lead-weighted belt to prevent them from floating off the bike as they pedal through the water and attempt to complete two lengths. Extra tall riders may have an advantage if their head is above the surface but for the average sized person the view is limited and they struggle to complete the Herculean task underwater.

The winner proves his or herself to be supreme practitioner in a sport that is the cycling equivalent of wading through a vat of congealed oxtail soup.

Health Resort

Llanwrtyd Wells is tucked in a valley between the Cambrian Mountains and the Mynydd Epynt in one of few remaining wilderness areas in Britain. The 'well' in the town's name dates to the eighteenth century when the vicar discovered a foul-smelling spring. It flowed with the same type of healing sulphurous water that made Harrogate, Bath and Buxton such fashionable spas. Llanwrtyd Wells flourished as a resort for a time as the gentry flocked to take the waters. Today's visitors to the town might want to consider a session of bog snorkelling. Just think of all the health benefits...

Bottle-kicking and Hare Pie Scramble in Hallaton, Leicestershire

If the Anarchy Party were to sponsor a sporting event then bottle-kicking would be a contender. It is a game with no rules played over a 1.5-kilometre course by players who consider rugby a sport for wimps. Since 1796, on Easter Mondays villagers from Hallaton and its neighbour Medbourne gather for the bottle-kicking and hare pie scramble – a mammoth tussle for possession of three 4.5-litre wooden casks (bottles). The aim of the contest is for players to run, crawl, wriggle or employ any human-powered manoeuvre to carry the bottle past the stream that marks their respective village boundary. There is little actual kicking but plenty of scrumming and some nifty footwork. Before the battle of the bottle comes the scramble and that is where the hare pie stars.

A large rectangular pie (made of beef rather than hare) is ceremoniously carried in a procession from the Fox Inn to St Michael's church. Leading the parade is a character called 'the warrener' dressed in a medieval green robe and carrying a striped pole topped by a bronze hare. Following behind are two porters who carry the precious pie between them; the breadmaid, also dressed in medieval fashion, holds a basket full of bread rolls or 'penny loaves' to distribute later; three men who march purposefully each holding a 'bottle'; and hundreds of spectators to complete the party. At the church gates the vicar blesses the pie and then cuts hunks off to throw towards a throng of outstretched arms.

The procession continues to the summit of a nearby hill known as Hare Pie Bank. Before combat begins, the remaining pieces of pie are up for grabs with everyone scrambling for morsels. Whether anyone eats it is debatable, although dogs are often spotted licking their chops.

Chief bottle-kicker, or master of the stowe, steps forward to perform his task. He picks up a bottle and throws it three times into the air. Only when it has hit the ground for the third time may play begin. 'Play' is a slightly misleading description: a veritable brawl ensues as dozens of players leap on the bottle in a chaotic scrum and retrievers try to grab it and throw it to a receiver on the edge of the swarm. Despite the name, the bottle is rarely kicked – being made of wood, whoever does kick it will know for a few days afterwards. If someone manages to filch the bottle and make a run towards their own village it is usually only seconds before they are brought down again. Ideally, a player breaks free of the tussle and sprints away. Or, more likely, the combined strength of a team overpowers the other and manages by the aid of brawn to inch its way home.

When a player crosses his village boundary in possession of a bottle his team keeps it and the next game begins. The winning team is the first to claim two bottles. It can take hours to conclude a game and as there are no rules, players drop in and out as they please, sometimes nipping off for refreshment (or alcohol anaesthetic) before returning to the melee.

By the end of play both teams are normally so muddy that no one can see the bruises. They trudge back to Hallaton for a final ritual in which players climb to the top of the Buttercross and drink beer from the bottles. Then it is off to the pub for a big celebration.

What is a Buttercross?

Many towns and villages have a buttercross. They used to be focal points in a marketplace where dairy producers gathered to sell cheese and butter from baskets. In some places buttercrosses are open-sided buildings that offer shelter but Hallaton's version is a solid conical structure on the village green around which merchants gathered to sell their wares.

SPORTING LIFE

Gurning World Championship in Egremont, Cumbria

'He had a face only a mother could love.' That phrase could well be the motto of a champion gurner and though it is normally used pejoratively, in gurning terms it is a huge compliment. Gurning is the art of pulling grotesque faces and it reaches exalted status at the World Gurning Championship in Egremont. To do it correctly the grimace must be framed by a braffin (leather horse collar) worn around the head. An ever-popular gurn is the pose perfected by people who remove their false teeth and have a face so rubbery they can cover their entire nose with their bottom lip.

Gurning competitions were once a common rural English tradition and some villages still continue the practice, though none is as celebrated as the contest that takes place during Egremont Crab Fair and Sports. As befits a World Championship, competitors come from many countries to showcase their most contorted expression. But no one from overseas has ever won because English men, women and children dominate this sport. In order to challenge for the title strict rules must be observed:

1. Before going on stage contestants may apply a little make-up and remove or reverse dentures.

2. Contestants stand on stage and hold the braffin so their head pokes through and can be seen clearly by the audience.

3. Contestants may not use hands or artifical aids to distort their faces.

4. Contestants may add dramatic effects to the performance by making wild animal-like noises.

A person need not be ugly to begin with because judges award marks to the entrant deemed to have changed their facial features most completely. Just watch out in case the wind changes direction.

The Origins of Gurning

The *Oxford Dictionary of English* suggests the word 'gurn' may originally be Scottish and related to 'grin'; whereas *The English Dialect Dictionary,* compiled by Joseph Wright, defines it as: 'to snarl as a dog; to look savage; to distort the countenance'. Many old customs have an unknown provenance and gurning is no exception. There is a theory that it originated in the habit of mocking the village idiot by throwing a horse collar around his neck. Today that mockery is a great accolade – in Egremont at least.

As in any sport a gurning championship contender needs to train. Two essential qualities for a successful gurner is facial malleability and not being afraid of scaring the neighbours. Top tips for improving the technique are: always practise in front of a mirror, concentrate and try to imagine living permanently with the grimace so it becomes second nature. Then attempt to make it look even worse. One family, the Mattinsons of Aspatria, claims two world-class gurners – Gordon and his son Tommy have claimed the men's World Gurning Championship multiple times.

One former winner hung up his braffin aged eighty-eight after seven decades of competing. His talents had improved with age. In what other sport do false teeth and sagging muscles afford such an advantage?

Egremont hosts its annual crab fair in September – an ancient celebration of the harvest that dates from 1267. The title has nothing to do with Crustacea; rather it refers to the crab apples that by tradition the lord of Egremont gave away to fair-goers. Throwing apples to the crowd from a cart as it trundles down Main Street is still a popular activity in the fair, although sweet eating apples have replaced the face-numbing sour crab version.

Whilst gurning is the highlight of the fair there are a number of other events. Cumberland wrestling is a regional speciality thought to have been introduced by tenth-century Vikings. Matches are always played on grass. At the start of the bout the two players 'tekk hod' (take hold), linking their fingers together behind the opponent's back. Players aim to lift up their rival and throw him to the ground so he lands face up. Something for everyone is dialect singing and it involves the recital of hunting, comic or sentimental songs in West Cumbrian dialect. But only the most determined should attempt another great traditional Egremont sport; that is, to climb the greasy pole and win a leg of lamb awarded to the person who reaches the top.

Crab Apple Jelly

Only people with the hardiest tongues could eat a raw crab apple without their face screwing up. But crab apple jelly made with plenty of sugar is sublime spread over warm scones and served with a pot of Earl Grey.

Haxey Hood in Haxey, Lincolnshire

As Christmas decorations are taken down around the country on 6 January, residents of Haxey are tearing across muddy fields in the annual tussle known as the Haxey Hood. This hood has nothing to do with headgear; rather, it is a piece of tightly rolled leather measuring 45 centimetres long and 8 centimetres in diameter. The objective is for players to move the hood from a field outside the village into their favourite pub. This is anything but easy as the brute force of a hundred-strong rugby scrum must be overcome. Throwing or kicking the hood is not permitted – just pushing and pulling.

Local folklore places the origins of the game sometime in the fourteenth century. Lady de Mowbray, wife of a local landowner, was out riding one day when a gust of wind blew her red silk hood into a field where it became 'boggined' (bogged down) in the mud. A group of farm labourers chased after it as the breeze whipped the hood away. Someone managed to grab it but he was shy and asked a friend instead to return the lady's property. Lady de Mowbray thanked the friend, saying he had acted like a lord and referred to the timid one as a fool. Her ladyship had enjoyed watching the pell-mell as the men ran after her hat and instructed them to restage the event the following year, each playing a specific role – lord of the hood, the fool and eleven boggins.

Over time the game has evolved but at its heart are modern-day representatives of the original thirteen peasants and they have a hoot performing their official duties. Lord of the hood and chief boggin both wear red hunting coats and top hats decorated with badges and flowers. The lord carries a 1.5-metre staff of office made up of thirteen willow wands bound thirteen times with willow twigs and topped with a red ribbon. The fool smears his face with red ochre and soot and wears a feathered hat studded with badges and a suit covered with multicoloured strips of fabric.

Before the game begins the officials take a tour of the village pubs to sing popular folk tunes including 'John Barleycorn' and 'Drink Old England Dry'.

In the afternoon they lead a procession of followers through the streets where the fool exercises his right for that day only to kiss all the women he meets. Outside the parish church the fool stands on a stone mounting block and proclaims a welcome that ends with a motto chanted by the crowds: 'Hoose agen hoose, toon agen toon, if tha meets a man nok im doon, but doant 'ot im'. Translation: house against house, town against town, if you meet a man, knock him down but don't hurt him.

Someone lights a pile of damp straw behind the fool for a ritual called 'smoking of the fool'. His predecessors would have been suspended from a tree branch and swung over a fire until the rope was cut and the hapless man fell into the flames. But not these days. A fit of coughing perhaps, third degree burns definitely not.

Ancient Farming System

Haxey is one of few remaining parishes where remnants of the medieval open field farming can be seen. Under this system each village was surrounded by several large unfenced fields divided into strips for individual subsistence farming. If the local landscape were enclosed by walls or hedgerows the Haxey Hood game would be impossible to play.

The game is open to anyone and there are no organised teams. Action begins when the hood is thrown into the air and a crowd of about two hundred players swarms to capture it and form a scrum, or in Haxey parlance a sway. The lord acts as referee and boggins help to extricate players from the mud when the sway collapses on top of them. This is no game for anyone with commitment issues – progress is slow and it can last for hours. Sometimes it looks as though little is happening apart from the sway heaving a little this way and leaning a bit that way. It is game over when the hood is deposited on the doorstep of one of the village pubs and ritually acknowledged by the landlord. Then beer is poured over the leather totem for luck and it is hung behind the bar, where it stays for a year until the next Haxey Hood.

Mad Maldon Mud Race in Maldon, Essex

Depending on a person's preference for cooking or cleaning they will either know Maldon for exceptional sea salt or for its glorious mud. The latter is the star of the annual Mad Maldon Mud Race, an event which lures people out of their New Year torpor to compete on the dirtiest racecourse imaginable.

Maldon is situated at the head of the Blackwater Estuary and when the tide goes out it *really* goes out, exposing acres of black, gooey sludge. That did not stop the Vikings though; they arrived in town during the reign of Ethelred the Unready and beat the Saxons at the Battle of Maldon in 991.

For the Mud Race, competitors chase through the cold water of the river Blackwater at low tide and up a slimy steep bank to the finish line. It may sound easy, but prior intentions to sprint may be dashed when the reality of the adhesive nature of the mud sinks in. Entrants are more likely to crawl and emerge at the end resembling the hippopotamus from the eponymous song by Flanders and Swann.

Around two hundred people normally enter the race, the majority of them in fancy dress and raising funds for charity. To avoid being trampled by the mob the trick is to start the race quickly and traverse virgin mud – it is much more challenging when it has been churned up by groups of drunken bearded chaps in pink wigs and the person dragging that inflatable palm tree behind them.

A tip from the experts to competitors is to wear gloves to protect the hands from concealed sharp stones when they are on all fours, as they almost certainly will be. Seasoned racers do not wear wellies, instead they tape trainers to their feet to prevent them from being sucked into the quagmire. Everyone is a potential winner in this race – even if an entrant comes last they may still win a prize for best costume. And the crowd of several thousand spectators will still cheer them as though they are world champs.

Black Water

The name of the estuary is nothing to do with all that mud discolouring the water. It derives from 'brackwater', meaning salty water. And sea salt is what Maldon is best known for.

Pic-Olym Games, countrywide

It is doubtful that Pierre de Coubertin was sitting in the boozer when he dreamed up the modern Olympics Games. If he had then perhaps latter-day athletes would be awarded medals for walking the plank rather than competing for gold in the high dive, or coming first in the pancake race instead of the 100-metre sprint. Unlike the aristocratic de Coubertin, Britain's sports visionaries have the pub to inspire them and many a genius idea has been concocted between friends over a pint.

Although the following assortment of world championship sporting events will never be included in the Olympics, they most certainly warrant being part of the Pic-Olym Games (a term devised by the author), a competition that does not exist. Yet unlike the Olympic Games, in the Pic-Olyms there would be no drug scandals, no political boycotts and no multi-billion pound infrastructure budgets. But the glory of coming top would still be priceless. And in place of an olive wreath medal winners might instead be honoured with garlands of horse chestnuts around the neck and a silver tankard stuffed with lettuce leaves – prizes at the World Conker Championships and the World Snail Racing Championship.

In no order of preference here is a variety of sports that should be included in an inaugural Pic-Olym Games.

World Coal Carrying Championship in Gawthorpe, West Yorkshire

Where else but a former coal mining village would host the World Coal Carrying Championship? It happens each year in

Gawthorpe on Easter Sunday and arose from a challenge by two friends in a pub to carry a sack of coal up a local hill and see who was fittest. That was 1963. Since then it has evolved into an international showdown. Beefiness is an advantage because contestants must run for just over 1,000 metres laden with one hundredweight (50 kilograms) of coal. A record speed for 'humping the coil' is four minutes and six seconds.

The Black Stuff

Gawthorpe, near Wakefield, sits on top of the Yorkshire coalfield and its connection with the black stuff dates back as far as 1366, during the reign of Edward III. The inclusion of 'thorpe' in a place name is of Danish origin and means 'outlying farmstead'. Gawthorpe is one of few villages with a permanent maypole.

World Conker Championships in Ashton, Northamptonshire

Some schools have recently banned the playing of conkers for fear of being sued by parents whose offspring come home with a black eye. So for the hard-done-to child who cannot engage in the traditional playground game, liberation is just round the corner at the World Conker Championships. This contest is held every year on Ashton village green on the second Sunday in October. Competitors stand on white podiums to battle it out in classes for men, women and children. When a winner emerges they mount the conker throne for coronation with the conker crown and garlands of conkers are hung around their neck. All hail the Conqueror!

The name 'conkers' probably stems from 'conquerors', a pastime that was originally played with snail shells. This evolved via hazel and cobnuts into the game that is now played with horse chestnuts on a string, where players try to shatter their opponent's conker into pieces. Some people try to gain an advantage by hardening their weapons, despite it being against the spirit of the game. Methods include soaking conkers in salt water, vinegar or paraffin; coating them with clear nail varnish; baking them in the oven, or storing them in the dark for a few months.

Ashton thwarts any foul play by supplying competition conkers ready drilled and laced. A number of rules govern the match including one that states: 'Each attempted strike must be clearly aimed at the nut, no deliberate miss hits.' No black eyes in Ashton then.

The National Woodland Inventory of Woodland Trees estimates there are 470,000 horse chestnut trees in Britain. No wonder, then, that so many world champions have been bred on British soil.

Football in the River in Bourton-on-the-Water, Gloucestershire

Rain never stops play at Bourton Rovers FC annual summer showdown because the match is played in the river Windrush that flows alongside Bourton's main street. Two teams of six take up position in 25 centimetres of water as hundreds of spectators line the banks and cheer on the players to score a goal through one of the arched stone footbridges. It is a splashy and boisterous game that lasts fifteen minutes each way, ending up as a good-humoured giant water fight.

Nicknamed 'Venice of the Cotswolds', Bourton-on-the-Water is so picture perfect that it is widely considered to be one of the prettiest villages in England.

Hen Racing World Championship in Bonsall, Derbyshire

Bonsall in the Derbyshire Dales is known internationally as a UFO hotspot with numerous sightings of flying objects that have no logical explanation. The village is also a poultry hotspot and leads the world in hen racing. At least, it does on the first Saturday in August when the World Championship Hen Races are run at the Barley Mow pub. Anyone with suitable fowl can enter the competition and be eligible for the triumph of owning the World's Fastest Hen, or take home prizes for Best Hen Deportment and Best Turned Out Hen.

Racing birds are placed in a 10-metre long chicken run and gently nudged as the commentator starts the race. And they're off! Slowly. A polite term to describe the athletes is absent-minded as they calmly strut and peck their way along the route, stopping sometimes to huddle, or turning and racing in the wrong direction. Spectators cheer on their chosen bird towards the finish line where children scatter corn to tempt the racers past the post so a winner can be declared. No hens were hurt in the making of this world championship.

Mascot Grand National in Huntingdon, Cambridgeshire

Huntingdon Racecourse is normally a forum where national hunt jockeys race the finest horses. Not during the Mascot Grand National. Then it is the turn of competitors such as Dazzler the Lion from Rushden and Diamonds FC, Swansea City's Cyril the Swan and Wacky Macky Bear of Saffron Walden FC to battle it out for top prize. Each year on the first Sunday in October approximately one hundred plush giant mascots belonging to sports teams and other organisations wobble (running is not an accurate description) along a one-furlong (200 metres) course and over six hurdles. Some cuddly toys romp home but others face the dastardly intervention of renegade mascots attempting to throw the race and are brought down. The race winner takes home a silver trophy but there are also prizes for: Best Turned Out Mascot, Ugliest Mascot (Captain Blade of Sheffield United and Graham the Gorilla of Finedon Volta FC are proud former recipients) and Oldest Mascot.

Pancake Race in Olney, Buckinghamshire

Pancake races happen all over the world on Shrove Tuesday but none like the traffic-stopping version in Olney. This is an all-female affair open only to Olney residents. Racers are required to wear the old-fashioned housewife costume of skirt, apron and headscarf but within that brief there is plenty of scope for fancy dress. Skirt lengths just above the knee are ideal as they do not impede running legs and speed is essential in this game.

Pancake tossers line up in Market Place outside the Bull Hotel. At 11.55 a.m. the starter instructs competitors: 'Toss your pancakes – are you ready?' Pan handles are firmly grasped and whoop – up go the pancakes, somersaulting before they flop back into the pan. Then the churchwarden rings the large bronze Pancake Bell and competitors sprint 380 metres to the parish church of St Peter and St Paul. The first woman over the finish line must toss her pancake again before she can be declared winner. When the race is completed the tossers enter St Peter and St Paul, place their frying pans around the baptismal font and sit in their special pew for a service.

Pancakes are traditionally eaten at Shrovetide and the custom of tossing them for pleasure dates back centuries.

Making pancakes was a way of using up perishable milk and eggs because the following day was Ash Wednesday, when a period of strict Lenten fasting began.

World Pea-Shooting Championship in Witcham, Cambridgeshire

Witcham becomes pea-shooting capital of the world for the annual championships at the village fair in July. A schoolmaster concocted the competition in 1971 when he confiscated pea-shooters from some naughty pupils.

Competitors must have their own peashooter but the organisers supply the peas. Peashooters can be made of any material and may even have telescopic sight devices, although the total length must not exceed 30 centimetres. Shooters stand 4 metres away from a putty target of concentric rings and fire. Peas make a depression in the putty and so scores are easily recorded. Contestants with the highest marks go forward into the pea-offs until all but one is knocked out – the new world champion.

Wheelbarrow Race in Ponteland, Tyne & Wear

The fastest wheelbarrow in the west (and north) is undoubtedly in Ponteland on New Year's Day. If ever a pastime could blow away the old year's dust, this is it. In a race for two people and one wheelbarrow; a team member sits in the barrow as the other one pushes as fast as they can without spilling the contents onto the road. Not easy if it has recently snowed. Anyone can enter, young and old: granddads pushing their grandchildren and vice versa have competed in the past. The dash starts outside the Blackbird Inn as the church bell strikes noon and it follows a circuitous route measuring almost 1.5 kilometres. Record speeds of just under eight minutes have been clocked.

World Pooh Sticks Championships in Little Wittenham, Oxfordshire

Are there any other world championships in which children compete equally with adults? Day's Lock on the river Thames is the site of the World Pooh Sticks Championships. Each year towards the end of March it attracts hundreds of entrants from Britain and overseas.

Pooh Sticks is the game beloved of Winnie the Pooh, Eeyore and Piglet. The original Pooh Sticks bridge, immortalised in the storybook *The House At Pooh Corner*, is in the village of Upper Hartfield near Tunbridge Wells. That region is an area of outstanding natural beauty called Ashdown Forest, a former royal deer-hunting ground, but now better known as Pooh Country.

A booklet called *The Official Pooh Corner Rules For Playing Poohsticks* was written by Mike Ridley in 1996 to commemorate the 70th anniversary of the publication of *Winnie-the-Pooh*. The rules include instructions for players to select a stick and show it to fellow competitors so the eventual winner can be identified. Players must stand side by side facing upstream as they hold their sticks at arm's length over the stream. After the starter says 'Go!' the sticks are dropped. Players then cross to the downstream side of the bridge and hope that their stick emerges first.

World Snail Racing Championships in Congham, Norfolk

Snail racing is not an oxymoron, and if proof were needed visit St Andrew's church fete when British garden snails compete in the world championship. The unbeaten record is held by a snail called Archie who in 1995 traversed a 33-centimetre racecourse in two minutes.

Anyone can enter a snail in the race, they just need to mark its shell with a number. Competitors place their mollusc in the middle of a damp paper circle and wait for the snail trainer to shout out: 'Ready, steady, slow!' A few minutes later a snail will cross the circumference finish line before any other, earning its handler a silver tankard stuffed with lettuce leaves.

At first sight the rule that no giant foreign snails may be entered might appear jingoistic but their size gives them an unfair advantage over the domestic common garden variety.

The Snail Trail

Congham's low-lying geography surrounded by ponds is ideal for snails and they flourish there. What racehorses are to Newmarket, snails are to Congham.

Surfing the Severn Tidal Bore, Gloucestershire

A dramatic natural phenomenon happens several times a month on the river Severn when the incoming tide forms a bore, a non-breaking wave that moves quickly upstream. It is caused by Atlantic tidal water entering the Bristol Channel and continuing up the Severn estuary. The water is filtered into a narrow conduit increasing the level by up to 15 metres, the world's second highest tide. As the river becomes shallower a mass of water builds up and attempts to overtake the leading wave, thereby forming a bore.

High spring tides are the most remarkable, when a bore can reach heights of 2 metres and move with an average speed of 16 kilometres per hour. No wonder, then, that such an amazing wave attracts surfers to ride one of the longest rollers in the world. The current record holder surfed for one hour and seventeen minutes, reaching speeds up to 20 kilometres per hour as he covered a distance of just over 12 kilometres.

Britain has a number of tidal bores: Solway Firth, Morecambe Bay and Trent Aegir on the river Trent in Lincolnshire. Some people claim that the tide King Canute failed to hold back was the Trent bore. But at least two other places also claim him: Bosham near Chichester, and Southampton. The latter is more likely as Canute was crowned King in the city in 1016. Canute was considered to be a wise ruler who has been misrepresented throughout history as a man with a monstrous ego who was so deluded that he believed even the sea would obey his decree. Instead, what he meant to prove were his limitations. He asked for his throne to be carried onto the seashore. There he sat as the tide advanced around him, ignoring the kingly command to halt. Canute was trying to illustrate that a king's authority was nothing in the face of God's power. Trouble is, he has been misconstrued and most people think he was a twit.

World Walking the Plank Championship in the Isle of Sheppey, Kent

Planker! That may sound like an insult but in fact it is the admiring soubriquet for people who compete in the annual 'walk the plank' contest at Queensborough Harbour on the Isle of Sheppey. Skills required for this sport are: dressing up in the most eye-catching costume and the ability to swim. The latter is essential because plankers are pushed off a wooden plank to the bottom of Davy Jones' locker by the fearsome cut-throat Captain Cutlass.

This August event attracts hundreds of landlubbers to watch as the Sheppey Pirates sail their galleon into harbour. Smoke, loud bangs, musket firing, and sword waving herald their arrival. Plankers line up to parade down the plank – a one-way journey – and impress the judges. Those connoisseurs of buccaneer style bestow scores for costume, use of piratical language, implementation of the jump and overall star quality. Successful candidates earn a certificate of welcome to Sheppey Pirates' Grand Order of World Class Plankers.

International Bognor Birdman in Bognor Regis, West Sussex

Breaking free from the shackles of gravity is the aim at the International Bognor Birdman Rally when competitors in human-powered flying machines attempt to flout the laws of physics. There is a substantial cash prize for flights over 100 metres but as yet it has never been claimed. In 2008 the festival was forced to change venue to Worthing because Bognor Regis pier, from which contestants launched themselves into the air, tumbling seconds later into the sea, was damaged and partially demolished.

Some people take the contest seriously and construct complex devices that incorporate wings, but the majority of competitors turn up in dressed as giant penguins, skateboarding cows, sugar plum fairies, pilots of magic flying carpets and innumerable other amusing get-ups. What they all have in common is the inevitable splash down. Isaac Newton was right.

> ## Britain's Olympics Influence
>
> Dr William Penny Brookes' Olympian Games at Much Wenlock in Shropshire is credited by Pierre de Coubertin as an inspiration for the modern Olympics and proof that his idea for an international contest could work in practice. Dr Brookes founded his version of the ancient competition in 1850 and later organised a national Olympian Games at Crystal Palace in 1866. The Wenlock Olympian Games are still an annual sporting event.

Robert Dover's Cotswolds Olimpick Games in Chipping Campden, Gloucestershire

Almost three centuries prior to the founding of the modern Olympics in 1894, a Cotswolds village was the centre of sporting excellence.

In 1612 a local lawyer called Robert Dover presided over the inaugural Cotswolds' Olimpick Games. The two-day event was quite a spectacle, attracting thousands of spectators to thrill at bouts of swordplay and throwing the sledgehammer. There was even a seventeenth-century equivalent of corporate boxes where the gentry was entertained in marquees away from hoi polloi. King James I gave instant credibility to Chipping Campden's homage to the games of ancient Greece when he granted them royal approval. Four centuries later Robert Dover's Cotswolds' Olimpicks in late May are still a highlight of the sporting calendar but unlike the international counterpart these games are an annual festival. If Robert Dover had chosen to clone the ancient Olympics a sacrifice of an hundred oxen would be required to honour Zeus. And lycra would have no place: athletes in the ancient games competed naked except in the contest where they had to race wearing armour.

When the British Olympic Association successfully bid to host the 2012 Olympics the official proposal acknowledged Robert Dover's innovation.

Dover's Hill is a natural amphitheatre that becomes a grassy stadium for the games. The opening ceremony takes place in front of a wooden stage-set depicting a castle and includes marching bands, cannon fire and a trumpet herald. Robert Dover and his friend Endymion Porter, played by two men on horseback dressed in seventeenth-century garb, declare the two-day event open.

There are two showgrounds: one for sports, the other for animal displays (such as falconry) and exhibition matches of backswords – a style of fencing where opponents each fight with a long and a short wooden stick.

The Championship of the Hill takes place in the sporting arena. Some events are already well known elsewhere: tug of war and standing jump. But others are less widely practised: shin-kicking, for instance. This is a form of wrestling played between two men dressed in white shepherd's smocks. In a best-of-three contest, players hold on to the opponent's shoulders and kick at their legs to weaken them before toppling them to the ground. Nowadays, players wear soft shoes and stuff their trousers with straw but in previous centuries no such protection was permitted and wrestlers could wear metal toe-capped boots. Ouch. Spurning the barre is similar to tossing the caber but is played with a shorter projectile. And the sack race is like no other; entrants are handicapped because the sack is tied at the neck, meaning competitors can't use their arms for balance and forward momentum.

All too soon the Olimpicks are over for another year. The closing ceremony is marked with a bonfire and fireworks on the hill and this is followed by a torchlight procession when several thousand people holding torches illuminate the darkness as they follow a marching band down to Chipping Campden town square. That is where the second part of the evening's festivities takes place, as pop bands perform into the night and people dance in the streets.

Nowadays the atmosphere at the Cotswolds' Olimpick Games is lively and people are generally orderly. But in the 1830s the occasion attracted crowds of up to 30,000 spectators, not all of whom watched quietly. Rowdy behaviour and drunkenness was the reason the games were eventually suppressed. But the annual sporting jamboree was too special to prohibit forever and in the early 1960s 'Robert Dover' in his feather-trimmed hat and ruffs once again proclaimed the games open.

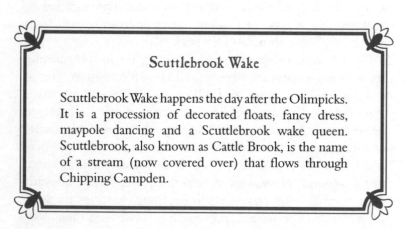

Scuttlebrook Wake

Scuttlebrook Wake happens the day after the Olimpicks. It is a procession of decorated floats, fancy dress, maypole dancing and a Scuttlebrook wake queen. Scuttlebrook, also known as Cattle Brook, is the name of a stream (now covered over) that flows through Chipping Campden.

Woolsack Races in Tetbury, Gloucestershire

How to impress the ladies in medieval Tetbury: hoist a heavy sack of wool onto your shoulders and race your friends up that very steep hill behind the village. Such athletic prowess is bound to astonish the females. Or so the local sheep drovers intended. Little did they know that centuries later their testosterone-led pastime would become a world championship, let alone one with equal opportunities, including races for both strapping lads and lasses.

The competition, on Spring Bank Holiday Monday at the end of May, is open to anyone and although there are few practical opportunities for training with a sack of wool, running up and down staircases with a small child on the back is a good start. Custom-made woolsacks weigh just under 30 kilograms for the men's race and 16 kilograms for the women and youths'. The racecourse itself is on Gumstool Hill with a sharp one-in-four gradient that runs for 240 metres down the street between the Royal Oak and Crown pubs. Competitors in each class line up at the top of the hill then hoist the deadweight onto their shoulders and sprint as fast as they can. Momentum carries them forward downhill but when it comes to the return journey, it's brutal. Knees buckle and the heart pounds until the shoulders are liberated from the load. All that effort is rewarded though, because the crowd lining the street cheers on each contestant as a hero.

Tetbury's extreme sport event may have echoes of the medieval period when the town was at the centre of England's most lucrative wool-producing area, but it is a recent invention dating back little more than thirty years. It can confidently style itself a world championship because one year a brigade of Nepali soldiers from the Ghurka Rifles won the men's relay event.

Some people rise to a challenge, and none more so than the competitor who once completed the course with the wool sack over his shoulders whilst riding a unicycle. Now that takes brawn *and* balance.

Cotswolds Wool

In the Middle Ages the Cotswolds were renowned as a source of some of the world's finest wool. Monasteries raised huge flocks of Cotswold Lions – native sheep with long golden fleeces. At that time wool accounted for fifty per cent of England's exports and underpinned the economy. Tetbury was situated near to a major east–west trade route (Oxford to Bristol) and was surrounded by drovers' trails, so it became an important marketplace for wool and yarn.

An ingenious method of increasing consumption of wool was introduced in the reign of Charles II. The Burial in Wool Acts of 1667 and 1678 (repealed in 1814) decreed that all bodies were to be buried in wool unless they had died from the plague. Or in the language of the law: 'No corps should be buried in anything other than what is made of sheep's wool only; or put into any coffin lined or faced with any material but sheep's wool, on pain of forfeiture of £5.'

Worm Charming World Championships in Willaston, Cheshire

Worm whisperers of the world gather at Willaston each year in June to compete in the World Worm Charming Championships, during which contestants show off their special techniques for encouraging earthworms to wriggle to the surface of the grass. Only vibrations may be used to lure annelids into the fresh air, and over the years twanging (a South Cheshire term) has been the most successful method for a big haul of worms. It entails quivering a four-pronged garden fork inserted approximately 15 centimetres into the turf. The person who collects the highest number of worms is the winner.

The International Federation of Charming Worms and Allied Pastimes adjudicates the competition at Willaston County Primary School in a worm arena that consists of 144 plots. Strict competition rules regulate the action. These include:

1. Lots are drawn to allocate plots.

2. Each competitor operates in a 1-metre square plot.

3. Competitors must keep clear of competition plots until instructed to 'Get to your Plots.'

4. Duration of competition is thirty minutes.

5. Worms may not be dug from the ground. Vibrations only to be employed.

6. No drugs may be used. Water is considered to be a drug/stimulant.

7. Music may be used to charm the worms out of the earth.

8. A garden fork may be stuck into the ground and vibrated by any manual means.

9. A piece of wood may be used to strike the handle of the garden fork to assist vibration.

10. Each competitor may collect worms from his/her plot only.

11. Competitors who do not wish to handle worms may appoint someone to do so. They are known as a 'Gillie'.

12. Worms must be handled carefully, collected in damp peat and placed in a container provided by organisers.

13. The competitor who 'charms' the most worms is the winner.

14. In the event of a tie the winner is decided by a further five minutes charming.

15. Worms are to be released into the wild after the birds have gone to roost on the evening of the event.

The prize for the most worms charmed is a trophy in the shape of a golden worm rampant. A silver trophy goes to the competitor who charms the heaviest worm. At the time of writing Tom Shufflebotham holds the record for the most worms ever charmed. He collected 511 in 1980, the first year of the contest, a feat later verified by the *Guinness World Records* book. The heaviest worm recorded so far weighed 6.6 grams.

As befits a championship open to international contestants, competition rules are available on the official website in over thirty different languages, including Latin. *Veni vidi duxi.*

Willaston's global worm challenge has a rival in Blackawton, Devon. Since 1984 the International Festival of Worm Charming has taken place each year in May. Several hundred charmers, many in fancy dress, parade through the village before getting down to business in a cow field. Blackawton's jamboree is more freestyle than the one in Cheshire in that competitors can use a variety of tools to encourage worms to the surface. Any liquid enticement is permitted providing the entrant tastes it first to prove it is not detrimental to creatures in the ground. Combinations of beer, gravy and sugar have been used to great effect in the past. Although the worm catch at Blackawton may not yet have matched Willaston's record, the Devonshire competition has something that the other one does not – a judge who farms worms for a living – the type that devours household waste and transforms it into natural fertiliser.

Earthworm Facts

- Common earthworms (*Lumbricus terrestris*) live at depths of up to 2 metres and feed on decaying organic matter in the soil.

- They help to fertilise soil by bringing nutrients closer to the surface.

- Worm casts are made up of excreted organic matter and are rich in nutrients.

- Earthworms are made up of 'annuli' – ring-like segments covered in minute hairs that grip the soil as the worm moves through it.

- The clitellum is a smooth band that comprises about one third of the worm's length. It is responsible for secreting the sticky mucus that covers the surface of the worm.

- Earthworms are hermaphrodite, with male and female reproductive cells. But they cannot self-fertilise and must find a mate.

The People's Rights

In the days before property, gathering and boundary rights were legally formalised, 'the people' lived under the threat of their rights being rescinded on a whim by the king, or those of a higher social standing than themselves. Charters guaranteed certain liberties and to this day it is cause for celebration to commemorate those hard-won common rights.

Boundary and Land Rights

Beating the Bounds, countrywide

Rogationtide is not a commonly used word except in a church. It stems from the Latin verb *rogare* 'to ask' and refers to a festival during which the faithful beseech God to bless the land, and ensure sun, rain and a good harvest. Rogationtide is just before Ascension Day (forty days after Easter Sunday) and incorporates a custom called 'beating the bounds' or 'riding the marches'. Before maps or surveys formalised boundaries villagers would walk around the parish once a year to maintain the integrity of the borders and prevent encroachment by neighbouring settlements. There was a practical element too because church finances from taxes and tithes were calculated on a parish basis, so knowing who lived where was more than just nosiness.

Stone markers (the marches) usually determined village limits. When the procession reached a marker a group of boys stepped forward and violently beat the bound (a term used for a marker stone; it derives from the word boundary) with willow branches. In some cases boys were whipped or tipped upside down, held by the ankles and their heads bumped against the stone. The idea was that such brutality would stick in a child's memory and so they would always remember the location of the boundaries. Some parishes still beat the bounds, but thankfully without the child abuse. One of the most dramatic beating-the-bounds rituals takes place in the shadow of the Tower of London.

Until the nineteenth century the Tower and a surrounding area known as Tower Liberty was outside the City of London's jurisdiction. Every three years on Ascension Day the Tower boundaries are checked. Players in this rite are the chaplain, choir boys and girls carrying willow wands, and officers of the Tower including the Chief Yeoman Warder holding the Mace, the Yeoman Gaoler carrying an execution axe, and two Yeoman Warders wearing scarlet and gold Tudor state dress. Thirty-one stones mark Tower Liberty's boundary, each painted with a red arrow upon a white background. As the group approaches a marker the chaplain proclaims, 'Cursed be he who removeth his neighbour's landmark,' and the children whack it a few times with their sticks and everyone shouts 'Marked!' In the case of a stone being in the middle of a busy road the Chief Yeoman Warder points the Mace towards it and hollers, 'Mark it well'.

Meanwhile, the neighbouring church of All Hallows-by-the-Tower church is also beating the bounds of its parish. All Hallows' group of officials – dressed in their robes and chains of office – consists of clergy, the alderman of Tower Ward and masters of livery companies connected with the church. The south boundary of All Hallows' is mid-stream in the river Thames so the group boards a boat to whip the marker.

All Hallows shares a boundary stone with Tower Liberty. In the past this disputed piece of land caused problems, culminating in a riot in 1698 between residents of the Tower and All Hallows' parishioners. Passions in the parish must have run high for them to risk a fight with the best-equipped fortress in the land. That demonstration is commemorated in a ceremonial exchange between the Tower governor and the vicar. The two groups meet at 7 p.m. by the contested marker on Tower Hill and the principals greet each other as follows:

Tower Governor:

Vicar of All Hallows, Alderman and Common Councilmen of Tower Ward, we salute you. On this Ascension Day evening

*we have come to beat the bounds of Her Majesty's Tower
Liberty. We greet our neighbours of All Hallows and assure
them that unlike our predecessors of 300 years ago we come
in peace. We are united in our efforts to maintain Tower Hill
as an historic open space.*

Vicar of All Hallows:

*Resident Governor, Yeomen Warders and people of the
Tower, we bring you greetings from the City of London and
the people of All Hallows. As we complete our own Beating
of the Bounds we greet you in peace and will unite our efforts
to yours in making Tower Hill a true meeting place for
all people of peace.*

Then both parties offer a salute to the Queen and disperse
without a punch being thrown.

Compared to Tower Liberty, checking the parish boundaries
of St Michael at the North Gate in Oxford is a trickier job,
but with no chance of insurrection. The tower of St Michael's
church is believed to be the city's oldest building, dating from
the Saxon period (circa 1040) when Oxford was a walled
settlement entered through east, west and north gates. Today
St Michael's is surrounded by commercial properties, many of
which conceal the boundary markers. Weeks before Ascension
Day the vicar writes to the owners of those businesses requesting
permission to mark the stones.

On the day everyone involved dresses in their uniforms
– university lecturers in academic gowns, the mayor in the
regalia of office, choristers in red surplices. All follow the
vicar, who's wearing a dog collar and holds aloft a large silver
and black cross. Where the stone markers are outdoors it is
simple to chalk the words 'St Michael at the North Gate (and
the year)' then it is thrashed with wooden sticks as everyone

choruses 'Mark! Mark! Mark!' If the marker is indoors it is not as straightforward. In Marks & Spencer, for instance, the boundary stone was removed when the shop was built. However, a condition of the planning permission was that the site would be preserved and so a metal cross was built into the floor. The procession meanders through the store trying not to knock ladies' underwear off hangers and assembles around the cross to give it a subdued whipping. Markers are also hidden in Littlewoods' loading bay, under a pub carpet, and in a storage area of the covered market. Lincoln College is built around the site of the final marker. The boundary beaters are invited to lunch there and are offered a glass of ivy beer (a secret college recipe of bitter ale infused with ground ivy), served only on Ascension Day.

Lichfield's Sheriff's Ride can accurately be described as a riding of the marches because up to 150 people on horseback join the annual perambulation of the 26-kilometre city boundary. It takes place on the Saturday nearest to 8 September and commemorates Queen Mary's charter of 1553 when Lichfield was detached from Staffordshire to form a separate county with the right to appoint its own sheriff. In the charter the sheriff was commanded to perambulate the city annually on the feast of the Nativity of the Blessed Virgin Mary.

The procession commences at 10.30 a.m. from Lichfield's guildhall and for the next eight hours it follows the boundary with stops for lunch, tea and a few horse races in between. After a glorious day out in the countryside the equine parade returns to Lichfield cathedral to be blessed by the dean. Lichfield's medieval cathedral is unique for having three spires, colloquially known as 'the ladies of the vale'.

Origins of Beating the Bounds

Beating of the bounds was a common custom in the Anglo Saxon period, sanctioned by the laws of Athelstan and Alfred the Great. The practice may stem from a Roman festival in honour of Terminus, the god of landmarks. At a *Terminalia* celebrants participated in dancing and sports on the boundaries of settlements and offered cakes and wine to the deity.

Dunting the Stone in Newbiggin, Northumberland

Once upon a time Newbiggin-by-the-Sea was such an important seaport that it was said to be third only to London and Hull in the export of grain. Being a freeholder in Newbiggin came with valuable rights – not least the entitlement to collect tolls from ships that used the harbour. Nowadays the seventy-seven existing freeholders cannot claim such taxes but they still own 185 acres of land on Newbiggin Moor including the local golf course, and are also joint owners of the foreshore along with the Crown.

In commemoration of historic rights dating to a charter in 1235, the freeholders gather on the Wednesday nearest to 28 May for the annual ritual of beating the bounds. Originally it would have been carried out on horseback with a bagpiper but today the landowners have a bracing walk instead.

The position of freeholder is bequeathed through generations so whenever a new member joins they go through an initiation ceremony called Dunting the Stone. It happens out in the open on the edge of the golf course. The two oldest freeholders hoist the newest by the feet and shoulders and bump his or her bottom three times on a lump of rock called the Dunting Stone. At the same time the secretary of Newbiggin Freeholders' Trust proclaims a formal greeting in archaic language and welcomes the new member, pointing out that since they have just been dunted then the privileges due to a lord of the manor are duly granted.

Afterwards the rookie freeholder should still be in a fit state to continue the walk around the land with its views over a beautiful beach on the North Sea coast.

The Front Line

The Northumbrian aristocracy once wielded immense power in English affairs. In their role as lords of the marches they protected England from Scottish invasion and bandit incursions in the fractious border region. That is the reason there are more defensive castles in Northumberland than any other county in England. By the fourteenth century Newbiggin was an important maritime centre called on by Edward III for support in the never ending military campaigns against the Scots.

Today Northumberland is England's least populated county and largely rural. Hard to believe that such a tranquil landscape was for centuries the scene of such violence.

Ancient Charters

Grovely Procession in Great Wishford, Wiltshire

Great Wishford's foolproof wake-up call is triggered as dawn breaks on 29 May. That's when a rough band performs its annual concert in celebration of Oak Apple Day. Describing their recital as music is hardly accurate – it's more a cacophony. The players set out to create a hullabaloo with dustbin lids, tin trays, saucepans banged with spoons, hunting horns and whistles in order to summon villagers to participate in the Grovely Procession. If percussion does not do the trick then repeatedly hollering the motto 'Grovely! Grovely! Grovely! And all Grovely!' usually works.

When everyone has gathered they walk up the hill into Grovely Woods and collect tree boughs to assert their ancient rights to gather wood for the coming year. When they have each picked up a branch they return to the village and hang them outside their homes as decoration. A branch known as the Marriage Bough is decorated with ribbons and hauled up to the top of St Giles' church tower. Good fortune will come to all who marry there in the following months. The most attractive boughs are entered into competition for a chance to win the Best Bough Cup. Serious contenders must be well-formed and ideally display oak apples – knobbly growths that are the dens of gall wasps rather than fruit.

Before gas and electricity powered our lives, gathering wood for fuel was essential. But many landowners treated timber as a commercial asset and strictly regulated access to woodlands. Great Wishford residents were fortunate – a charter of 1603 formalised in law the villagers' rights to collect wood. The charter stipulates that residents must go to Salisbury Cathedral to perform a dance and 'there make claim to their customs in the Forest of Grovely in these words: "Grovely, Grovely, Grovely. And all Grovely!"'

After breakfast, villagers travel to the cathedral and fulfil the words of the Charter. Their predecessors walked to Salisbury and naturally had to stop frequently along the way for libations. At some point in the nineteenth century villagers were banned from the cathedral on Oak Apple Day for being too merry. That meant an important element of the annual ritual died out. It was resurrected in the 1960s and now villagers, on their best behaviour, many of them in historic costume, gather on the cathedral green. They form a procession with someone carrying the Oak Apple flag and the Oak Apple banner bearing the motto: 'Grovely, Grovely, Grovely. And all Grovely! Unity is strength.'

Four dancing ladies are dressed in long dark skirts, aprons and bonnets – clothes worn in tribute to Grace Reed, who was jailed in 1825 for entering Grovely Woods. Her crime was to look for kindling after her village Barford St Martin had relinquished collecting rights in return for an annual payment of coal. The dancers perform two square dances with music provided by a villager in a traditional smock and playing a melodeon. For one dance they hold oak twigs and in the other dance bundles of sticks known locally as nitches tied together with a spray of green leaves. Afterwards everyone is invited into the cathedral to approach the altar. The rector recites a section of the charter and the throng asserts Great Wishford's land rights by shouting as loudly as they can: 'Grovely, Grovely, Grovely. And all Grovely!'

With the ceremony completed the group can return to the village for a special lunch in a marquee. In the afternoon the May queen and her attendants join a parade of floats, morris dancers and a marching band to Oak Apple Field where the local school children show off their maypole dancing skills at a celebratory fete.

Over centuries the villagers of Great Wishford had to protect their entitlement through numerous disputes between them and the lord of the manor. In 1892 the Wishford Oak Apple Club was established to defend the Grovely rights. It was only in 1987 that a new accord recognised the villagers' full privileges. Although no one now depends on wood for cooking and heating, the club continues to safeguard the traditions laid down in the Charter of 1603 as a principle for those rights that their ancestors struggled to win and intends to continue the Grovely Procession in perpetuity.

The Enclosures Acts

Enclosure was the process whereby the ancient open field system of arable farming in England and Wales was ended. Several Acts of Parliament between 1603 and 1903 made it legal for landowners to fence their land and take away traditional common grazing and collecting rights. Ostensibly, it was done to improve the productivity of farming land and many farmers benefited but those who did not were turned into landless labourers.

Hocktide Court Festival in Hungerford, Berkshire

John of Gaunt, Duke of Lancaster and the son of King Edward III, was largely reviled throughout England in the fourteenth century. But in Hungerford he was Sir Popular due to common grazing and fishing rights His Grace granted to the townsfolk. Such privileges were crucial to poor people who largely depended on the ability to rear or catch their own food. To legalise his gift he issued a charter and donated a hunting horn to the town. But at some time in the late sixteenth century someone stole the charter document at a time when the Duchy of Lancaster was attempting to claim back those valuable common rights. Much legal wrangling ensued and the matter was resolved in Hungerford's favour only when Queen Elizabeth I intervened.

Hungerford celebrates those historic entitlements on the second Tuesday after Easter when the town is decorated with blue and white ribbons for the Hocktide Court Festival. At 8 a.m. the town crier stands on the town hall balcony and rings a bell to signal the start of the annual ritual. The duke's hunting horn is blown to summon commoners of the court – they are the owners of 102 properties in the high street that come with commoners' rights attached to the freehold. Commoners who do not attend court are fined a penny or forfeit their rights for a year. Of all the commoners' rights today it is the fishing rights that are the most valuable – guests pay £50 a day to fish in the river Kennet and money raised from permits goes to the Hocktide Court charitable trust.

During the Hocktide Court session officers are elected with ancient titles that include portreeves, water bailiffs and tithing men. They each have a role in administering the common rights for the coming year. Two of them are nominated as 'tutti-men' and they have the most fun throughout the day. It is their job to visit commoners' houses to collect any outstanding dues. Men pay a penny and women must forfeit a kiss. But these are no ordinary debt collectors. For a start, they dress in morning coats, top hats and carry poles adorned with flowers, ribbons and crowned with a cloved orange. Accompanying them are tutti-wenches – girls from the local school – who wear a sixteenth-century costume of aprons and shawls and carry baskets of oranges to hand out to passers-by. The tutti-men are welcomed with generous hospitality wherever they go, usually in the form of a libation, and spend the day with a big grin on their faces.

After the business of court concludes it is time for lunch and toasting all present with warm punch. Then the town blacksmith enters the room, wearing his leather apron. He is there to 'shoe the colts'. He grabs the legs of any newcomers and hammers a horseshoe nail into the heel of their shoe until they shout 'Punch!' On that signal they are released with the proviso that they buy a round of drinks for everyone so the sociable celebration of John of Gaunt's philanthropy can continue.

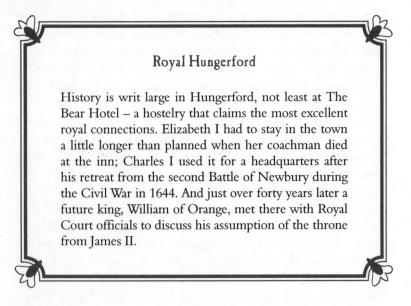

Royal Hungerford

History is writ large in Hungerford, not least at The Bear Hotel – a hostelry that claims the most excellent royal connections. Elizabeth I had to stay in the town a little longer than planned when her coachman died at the inn; Charles I used it for a headquarters after his retreat from the second Battle of Newbury during the Civil War in 1644. And just over forty years later a future king, William of Orange, met there with Royal Court officials to discuss his assumption of the throne from James II.

Rowell Charter Fair in Rothwell, Northamptonshire

Each year Rothwell marks the feast of Holy Trinity (eight weeks after Easter Sunday) with a five-day celebration to commemorate the Charter for an annual fair granted by King John in 1204. In medieval England, fairs were a combination of livestock markets and days of frivolity for the peasants, who were given the day off work. Today the only animals being traded are furry toy prizes on the sideshows, but the fair is still as popular.

Rothwell residents are so proud of the charter heritage that hundreds of them participate in an early morning event on Rowell Fair Monday. On that day the bailiff to the lord of the manor dons a morning suit and top hat and is hoisted onto the back of a shire horse. Surrounding him is a bodyguard of around twenty halberdiers, each carrying a halberd – a diamond-shaped metal spike mounted on a 10-metre long wooden pole. As the bell in the church tower chimes 6 a.m. a hunting horn wails. The Proclamation Ceremony begins and the bailiff, on horseback, reads aloud the Charter granted in 1614 by King James I:

Whereas heretofore his late majesty King James I and his progenitors Lords of the Manor of Rowell had and used to have one fair in the year to be holden within the said manor which said fair is now by good and lawful means come to [insert name of current Lord of the Manor]. He the said [insert name of current Lord of the Manor] doth by these presents notify and declare that the said fair shall begin this Monday after the feast of the Holy Trinity and so to continue for the space of five days next after the holding and keeping of it and no longer, during which time it shall be lawful for all Her Majesty's subjects to come and to go, to buy and to sell, all manner of cattle, merchandise and other stuff being saleable ware and allowed to be bought and sold by the laws of this kingdom. No toll for cattle, stakes for horses, sheep pens, shows and stalls are charged heretofore. And he further chargeth and commandeth all manner of persons within the liberties of the said fair to keep the Queen's peace in all things, upon such penalties as the laws and statutes of this kingdom are provided.

Then he declares: 'God save the Queen and the lord of the manor.' Quite a mouthful. But that is just a warm-up because the Bailiff then sets off on a crawl of the town's pubs and former pubs where he is duty bound at every location to proclaim the charter from the back of his mount. Not only that but the bailiff must drink a glass of rum and milk outside each hostelry – traditionally that cocktail was meant to keep away the morning chill. But what's this? A number of lads are trying to wrestle the halberdiers' weapons away from them. Police officers look on without reacting because it is a tradition for the youths to engage in this bruising horseplay after each reading of the charter.

It takes the bailiff about an hour to conclude the ceremony. Afterwards he returns to the pubs to say thank you, and it would be impolite to refuse another drink. By the end of the day's festivities he has probably consumed twenty glasses of milky rum. Good job the working horse's girth is so wide that it is difficult for the rider to fall off.

In addition to the Proclamation Ceremony the fair also includes the Celebration Parade of costumed historical characters led by the bailiff and halberdiers. Later there is the Pageant in the Park with a display of medieval knights in combat, and of course a fun fair.

One of the bailiff's jobs in previous centuries would have been to visit tenants and collect taxes for the lord of the manor. Today's bailiff organises the fair and then collects rent from the businesses involved. The money is passed to the current lord of the manor and profits are donated to charity.

A Rum and Milk a Day Keeps TB Away

According to *Cassell's Dictionary of Cooking* (1875) a glass of rum and milk: 'first thing in the morning or else twice a day is strongly recommended as of the greatest service in cases of consumption. It is often almost as efficacious as cod-liver oil.'

Lanimer Day in Lanark, Lanarkshire, Scotland

Pomp, horses, heralds, swords, a queen – sounds like a regular day out for the monarch. But in this case it is a celebration known as Lanimer Day when the town of Lanark checks its boundaries. Lanimer is a corruption of 'land march' and to the townsfolk of Lanark it means a big bash and several days of festivity in June. At the heart of Lanimer week is the ritual of checking fifteen stones that mark the parish limits. Town officials used to be paid to carry out this chore but nowadays it is done voluntarily with great pageantry and enjoyment. An official called Lord Cornet is the ceremonial leader – a great honour that lasts for a year.

Horsemanship is mandatory because the perambulation of the marches entails Lord Cornet leading a procession of riders around a route of almost 6 kilometres to check the northernmost march stones and ensure they are in position and do not need to be replaced. A crowd of hundreds follows on foot behind the horses. One of the stones is in the middle of a river so anyone who wades out to check its condition ends up soaked. After each stone in the area has been visited everyone returns to town for a ceremony called the Shifting of the Standard. The burgh standard is passed from the ex-Lord Cornet to the current holder with instructions to hand it on the following year 'unsullied and unstained'.

A check of the remaining marches is made during the Evening Ride Out. Past and present Lord Cornets and friends examine the markers to the south, east and west of the town. Then the horses are given a workout at Lanark racecourse in a series of races including one called the Burgh Spurs.

Lanark – Patriot Town

Lanark was the location of the first Scottish Parliament in 978 and later one-time home of William 'Braveheart' Wallace who first brandished a sword to free his native land in 1297 when he killed the town's English sheriff.

On Lanimer Day itself Lord Cornet and his retinue is escorted by a cavalcade from the Strathclyde Mounted Police to greet guests outside Memorial Hall where the Lord Provost of South Lanarkshire proposes a toast: 'Safe oot, safe in'. The riders trot off to meet hundreds of children, several pipe bands, numerous decorated floats and others gathered to participate in the Morning Procession and the Crowning of the Lanimer Queen. Every monarch has a court and this one is no exception. Up on a dais the queen's attendants comprise the queen's champion, first lord, second lord, two Yeomen of the Guard, two heralds, crown bearer, sceptre bearer, sword bearer, proclamation bearer, two page boys, four outriders, twelve ladies-in-waiting and two chief maids.

A final check of the march stones takes place during the Afternoon Ride Out followed by the Declaration at Lanark Cross – a report on the state of the boundary markers. When official business is concluded the Evening Spectacular gets underway with a military tattoo of marching bands and bagpipes. And finally, to the Lanimer Queen's Reception when her majesty presides over a display of singing and dancing by children who took part in the Morning Procession.

Lanark is unique in being the only burgh in Scotland that has checked its boundaries each year since it was granted burgh status in 1140 by King David I. A reminder of the historical necessity of checking them comes in the presence of the birks – townspeople who carry boughs of birch or willow along the procession route. The ritual commemorates a series of legal disputes prolonged over 150 years when local landowner, the Laird of Jerviswood, and his descendents tried to prevent anyone trespassing on their land. It culminated in 1840 with accusations that participants in the perambulation of the marches had damaged 300 birch saplings on land belonging to the laird. He claimed land that residents of Lanark considered to be within the parish boundary. The case dragged through the courts for eight years and Lanark council was about to concede defeat when someone checked the property records and discovered that the laird has never formally purchased the land in question. He lost the case. Power to the people!

Myths and Folklore

Many British traditions have been passed through the generations by word of mouth and their origins are unclear. Some theories explain them as metaphors for good versus evil or, in the case of people dressing up in costume to play certain characters, as representing scapegoats In modern-day Britain, where logic is supposed to prevail, it makes the events included in this chapter even more fascinating.

The Art of Disguise

Burry Man in South Queensferry, West Lothian, Scotland

Wearing a suit covered in thousands of scratchy burrs and walking around all day in it without sitting down is hardly taking it easy. John Nicol knows because he has played the role of Burry Man at South Queensferry's Ferry Festival Fair in early August several times over the years. So what is the Burry Man? Imagine a human-sized teddy bear but instead of fur it is covered in the spiky heads of the burdock plant – those hooked burrs that stick to clothing and passing animals (inspiration for the man who invented Velcro). Now picture the teddy bear wearing a yellow sash printed with an image of Scotland's red rampant lion, a hat decorated with fresh flowers, and carrying two staffs fashioned from ferns and other vegetation.

Three attendants accompany Burry Man – two that guide the way around town and one who rings a bell to signal his arrival. Burry Man walks with arms outstretched – he can't put them down because the burrs would stick together and prevent him from doing something very important – lifting a glass of whisky towards his lips. He stops first at the provost's house (a provost is the equivalent of a mayor) where he is offered a snifter of the water of life drunk with the help of a straw poked through a hole in the costume. This scene is repeated at pubs along the route and Burry Man is welcomed enthusiastically wherever he goes. It would be bad manners to refuse a drink and besides he cannot say no as it is tradition not to utter a word during the mammoth nine-hour ritual.

Playing the role of Burry Man is a great accolade. Only men born in South Queensferry are eligible and they are responsible for assembling their own costume. Before the festival the anointed one makes several forays into the countryside to search for burdock plants. He needs to collect at least 10,000 burrs. They are dried and meshed together to form twenty-five large patches. On the big day Burry Man is helped into his costume. He dons trousers and a shirt over which he pulls leggings and a long sleeved vest as protection against the unrelentingly abrasive burrs. Patches are attached to the over-garments until they envelop the entire body. A burr-covered full-face balaclava disguises the head and a flowery hat tops off the one-of-a-kind ensemble. And there he is – Burry Man now ready to parade around the village accepting hospitality from the locals and bringing good luck to those who meet him.

The Burry Man

Quite what Burry Man represents is not clear, though the custom dates back to at least 1687. Two theories appear most likely. The first suggests that Burry Man is a green man type character, a god of the land who represents fertility and vegetation. The second is that Burry Man is a scapegoat character who traipses around the village capturing evil spirits on the spiky burrs, and suffering his uncomfortable fate for the benefit of the community.

Wearing such a costume is deeply uncomfortable, sweaty, claustrophobic and prickly. But an incentive for the person underneath is the knowledge that they continue a centuries-old tradition, one greatly enjoyed by locals and visitors. Having

Burry Man on a CV is unique. And access to all the whisky you can drink – that can't be bad either.

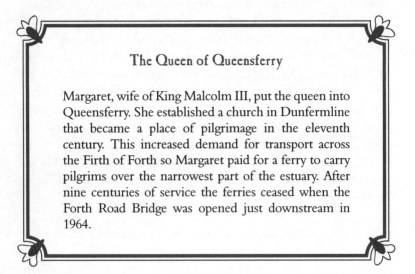

The Queen of Queensferry

Margaret, wife of King Malcolm III, put the queen into Queensferry. She established a church in Dunfermline that became a place of pilgrimage in the eleventh century. This increased demand for transport across the Firth of Forth so Margaret paid for a ferry to carry pilgrims over the narrowest part of the estuary. After nine centuries of service the ferries ceased when the Forth Road Bridge was opened just downstream in 1964.

Clown Church Service in Dalston, London

A costumed clown wobbling on a unicycle down the aisle is hardly a common sight in Anglican churches but a special dispensation is made each year on the first Sunday of February at Holy Trinity, Dalston. That day it becomes the clowns' church, although it is still open for anyone to worship in. Proof of its association with comic performers is a stained glass window that represents scenes in the life of Joseph Grimaldi, the celebrated eighteenth-century entertainer. He invented the white face paint and red cheek triangles that countless modern-day clowns still wear.

Since 1959 the Joseph Grimaldi Memorial Service has been a highlight of the clowning year. Jesters from all over the world, irrespective of their religious convictions, meet to give thanks for the gift of laughter. In 1967, when Clown Smokey persuaded church authorities to permit the clowns to attend in full motley and slap (costume and make-up), the event took on a surreal edge. Worshippers wearing face paint, red noses, polka dot bow ties and multi-coloured wigs throng the nave and attempt to fold their oversized shoes under the pews. Then they lift the rafters as they sing hymns and cheerily join in with the prayers. Eyes closed and this could be a regular church service. But it is not – where else would the vicar blow bubbles from the pulpit as the clowns' chaplain does?

Putting the Pun in Fun

Joseph Grimaldi, born of an Italian father in London 1778, used to pun, 'I am grim all day but I make you laugh at night!'

Hobby Horses in Padstow, Cornwall, and Minehead, Somerset

Hobby horses come in two guises – the benign wooden horse head on a pole beloved of Victorian children or the grotesque creature costumes that dance around the streets at festivals. Padstow in Cornwall celebrates May Day with its two unforgettable 'obby 'osses as horse fever infects everyone and the town stops still.

Padstow's labyrinth of crooked medieval lanes is decked with flags and the greenery of spring: bluebells, forget-me-nots, cowslips and tree catkins. The place is ready for its biggest party of the year. At midnight on the eve of May Day a group of 'mayers' commences the first rendition of the towns' special

May song. Over the subsequent twenty-four hours it will be sung hundreds of times. The following morning Old 'Oss and Blue Ribbon 'Oss are welcomed onto the streets with huge cheers from the crowd. The two 'horses' look similar – a 2-metre wide circular frame over which shiny black oilskin hangs so it resembles a huge lampshade. A stylised horse's head with snapping jaws on a long neck protrudes from the frame. A volunteer carries the contraption over his or her shoulders, wearing on the head a black and red striped conical hat topped with a horsehair tail, face hidden under a fearsome mask. Each 'oss is led by a character called the teaser carrying a painted club and accompanied by a group of supporters dressed in white with blue or red sashes. No May Day would be complete without music so a band of drummers and melodeons plays a lively rhythm as the procession meanders through town.

The 'osses tilt, twist, swoop and skip in an energetic rumba. Occasionally, the music slows and an 'oss sinks to the ground in melancholy as the Teaser strokes it with their club. Suddenly the beating drums reach a crescendo, the crowd cries "Oss, 'oss!' and the beast springs back up to continue dancing at a rapid pace. This spectacle continues for hours until the two 'osses meet at the maypole in the town square for a spirited *pas de deux*. Then with their annual outing at an end they are led back to their respective stables as the crowd belts out lyrics of the 'Farewell' song. The 'osses may have gone home but for everyone else the night is young and the atmosphere electric so there is nothing else for it but a visit to the pub to continue the party.

Minehead in Somerset has a similar May Day hobby horse. Like Padstow, this town also has two such characters. One is known as the Sailors' Horse and the other is the Town Horse. They both resemble the outline of a ship covered in canvas painted with multicoloured roundels and adorned with ribbons and strips of material. Dragging along behind is a long tail made up of colourful rags. A volunteer wears the 3-metre by 1-metre decorated frame, head obscured under a terrifying African style mask and a pointed hat. A shoulder plume of ostrich feathers completes the ornamentation. This horse is a mischievous creature swaggering through town to the beat of drums and the melody of accordions, shaking vigorously, scaring children, sidling up to women and waylaying the men. He often flicks unsuspecting spectators with his tail. And bystanders who fail to make a donation to the charity collection are liable to be 'booted', a punishment that entails being held face down and tapped several times on the backside by the hobby horse.

Beasts of Burden

The horses of Minehead are beasts of burden that work hard to spread their naughty charm each year from 30 April to 3 May. A local legend suggests that they originated when someone dressed up as a horrifying monster as a way of preventing Danes in the ninth century landing in town and causing trouble. Perhaps he represents the king of May. No one knows when or why the tradition began.

In the year 2000 someone in Banbury, Oxfordshire had the genius idea of hosting a hobby horse festival. After all, the town is known throughout the world for the nursery rhyme:

Ride a cock horse to Banbury Cross
To see a fine lady upon a white horse
With rings on her fingers and bells on her toes
She shall have music where ever she goes.

Each year in early July hobby horses of the world unite in Banbury to parade and race. All styles of horse are welcome and wicker, flower, metal, wooden and cloth models have entered in the past – including the classic Victorian children's version. Superstars of the genre have visited too, including a hobby horse called Sam from Ilmington Morris Men – at over one hundred years old, he's the country's oldest.

Ride a Cockhorse to Banbury Cross

Banbury is at the top of a hill so a cockhorse would have been very useful. Cockhorses were used *ad hoc* to provide extra power to haul carriages up steep slopes if the existing harness horses struggled with the load. At the summit it would be unhitched and ridden back down again to await the next customer.

Mari Lwyd in South Wales

Mari Lwyd is not a hobby horse, rather a real horse skull decorated with glass eyes, ribbons and bells. It is mounted on a wooden pole and carried by someone hiding under a white sheet. Macabre though it looks, the horse is a fun character at the centre of an old Welsh tradition now largely confined to Cardiff, Glamorgan and Llanwrtyd in Powys. During the Christmas season Mari Lwyd visits take place when the horse and her party – the leader, the sergeant and a couple of men dressed as women – tour the pubs and selected homes to sing traditional songs that ask for food and sustenance for the horse. Then comes the *pwnco* – a battle of wits where challenges and insults spoken in rhyme are exchanged with the Mari Lwyd party. A visit from Mari brings good luck so it makes sense to let her win the encounter.

Cwmni Caerdydd, Cardiff's Welsh folk dance troupe, recreates the tradition at the Old House pub in the village of Upper Llangynwyd on New Year's Eve day. It is not such a drink-soaked occasion as it was in the eighteenth and nineteenth centuries. The custom waned as church sermons railed against the 'pagan practice' and encouraged parishioners to resist the temptation to join in.

Little is known about the origins of the Mari Lwyd tradition. One theory suggests that it is a mid-winter ritual about the promise of rebirth in spring – in this case a dead horse brought back to life.

Hunting of the Earl of Rone in Combe Martin, Devon

Pity the poor Earl of Rone, a fugitive on the run from the massed villagers of Combe Martin. More efficient than bloodhounds, the locals relentlessly track their prey until he is cornered and arrested. But the Earl should be used to it by now because it happens each year over the spring bank holiday weekend.

Rowdy and licentious, the Hunting of the Rone was banned in 1837 but revived in 1974. Today it is a boisterous celebration with great opportunities for dressing up in character. There are several to choose from: the earl himself disguised in a sack outfit stuffed with straw, a necklace of ship's biscuits around his head and a grotesque mask obscuring his face. Another favourite is the hobby horse, this one resembling a colourful Mexican sombrero with legs. The fool pairs up with the hobby horse, a group of uniformed fake Grenadier Guards led by two drummers join in the fun and accordion players provide a traditional musical soundtrack.

Following the throng are girls and women dressed in a rural eighteenth-century costume of shawls and long skirts, and little boys in breeches and urchin caps. During the holiday weekend villagers band together to hunt for the earl – unsuccessfully until Monday night when two drummers lead the contingent of Grenadiers up to Lady Wood to poke around in search of the outlaw. He is finally apprehended hiding amongst the trees. His capturers inconsiderately plonk the earl sitting backwards on a donkey to be paraded through the village and down to the sea. At intervals the soldiers 'shoot' the earl, causing him to fall off his mount and lay dead in the street. Each time he is revived by the fool and the hobby horse and helped back on to the animal. When the earl reaches the beach his nine lives are over and the final shots kill him. That is the signal for villagers to start baying as the Grenadiers run into the water carrying an effigy of the Earl of Rone and fling it as far as they can out to sea. Everyone cheers as the figure floats away.

Combe Martin's very own manhunt has a long history, although it is not clear how far back it dates. Legend suggests it is based on the Earl of Tyrone who fled from Ireland in 1607 and was shipwrecked on the North Devon coast. He hid from search parties in woods around Combe Martin, surviving on ship's biscuits until a group of Grenadiers tracked him down. But that legend is not true. The real story concerns the Nine Year War that raged from 1594 to 1603 between Catholic Ireland and Protestant England. Senior commander Sir Hugh O'Neill, Earl of Tyrone, was forced to concede defeat but later reconciled with King James I. Unfortunately for the earl, he had too many enemies relentlessly plotting against him. Tyrone believed his arrest and probable execution was imminent and the only alternative was self-imposed exile. So the earl and a large group of Irish chieftains boarded a ship bound for continental Europe in what became known as the Flight of the Earls. Tyrone died in Rome in 1616.

Tyrone's flight was big news at the time so maybe villagers of Combe Martin were engaging in wishful thinking about capturing an enemy of the state when they enacted the Hunting of the Earl of Rone. What the custom really means or why it originated is a mystery. Some speculate that the Earl of Rone is a scapegoat figure, others that he is a version of the pagan green man. Perhaps the earl represents a local outlaw. But whatever he embodies, the modern-day villagers continue the tradition with gusto.

Was the Original Scapegoat Really a Goat?

Yes – in the Hebrew bible Aaron confesses the sins of the children of Israel over the head of a live goat. Then, as it symbolically bore everyone's transgressions, it was banished into the wilderness. An English translation of the bible in 1530 referred to 'a goat that departs' – this later became 'the goat that escapes'.

Mummers' Plays, countrywide

Ever wondered where the term 'keeping mum' originated? 'Mum' is a Middle English word for silent. That has nothing to do with mummers or mummers' plays, though. In that context the word 'mummer' likely derives from an early German word that translates as disguised person.

A Mummers' play is a ritual comic drama often performed at Christmas by mummers or guisers (actors in disguise) in the street or in a pub. Characters usually introduce themselves in rhyming couplets from traditional dialogue that has been around for years. Costumes are of the make-do-with-whatever-is-available variety plus cardboard props. The principal roles are: the hero – commonly St George or Robin Hood, the hero's opponent, sometimes known as the Turkish knight, the fool, the slasher, and always the quack doctor. A battle ensues and someone is killed – but lo! Here comes the doctor, loudly proclaiming his skills as a medic, curing all disease and casting out devils. He administers a magical tincture and always manages to restore life to the dead man. Just as it always should, good triumphs over evil.

Mummers' plays – sometimes known as plough plays or pace egging, depending on the region and what time of the year they are performed – originated in the Middle Ages. The current format dates to the eighteenth century and they were once commonly performed in villages all over Britain. Mumming was a lucrative hobby for poverty-stricken farm labourers who could earn the equivalent of a month's wages for just a few seasonal performances.

Several troupes keep the tradition alive, not least the Marshfield Mummers in Gloucestershire. Also known as the Old Time Paper Boys, their costumes are made up of newspaper strips sewn onto clothes and hats so their faces are concealed. Each Boxing Day a large crowd gathers at 11 a.m. in the market square to sing Christmas carols. Then the town crier in his official overcoat and top hat rings a hand bell: 'Oyez, oyez, I have much pleasure in introducing the celebrated Marshfield Mummers, the Old Time Paper Boys. God save the Queen!' At Marshfield the characters are: Father Christmas, King William, Little Man John, Doctor Phoenix, Saucy Jack, Tenpenny Nit and Father Beelzebub. Without warning, King William and Little Man John commence a vicious sword fight. But Little Man John does not stand a chance and is slain by the King. Cue the Doctor, who rushes to the rescue with his enchanted potion and miraculously brings the dead man back to life. The play is swiftly performed in several locations around the village including the Lord Nelson pub. Not more than an hour after they began it is over and the paper boys can pack the costumes away for another year.

Gloucestershire, Somerset and Avon are hot spots for mummers. The Weston Mummers near Bath give several performances in the region over Christmas; the Bishopswood Mummers perform at Christmas and also appear at wassails, mid-summer festivals, and autumn fairs; and the City of Gloucester Mummers present their play on Boxing Day outside the cathedral.

A closely related version of mumming is Cheshire souling or soul-caking plays. As the name suggests, they are performed to mark All Souls Day at the beginning of November. The theme of death and resurrection is central, with a battle between St George and the Turkish champion. But souling differs from mumming in its inclusion of a mischievous horse that is keen to cause havoc. Like the hobby horse, this equine character is a human in a black sheet and a decorated horse skull mask.

Painted Eggs

Pace Eggs (pace derives from *pascha* – Greek for Easter) are the hard-boiled eggs traditionally painted at Easter. In former centuries they were given as gifts to touring entertainers who became known as pace eggers – these were the Yorkshire and Lancashire versions of mumming troupes.

Straw Bear Festival in Whittlesey, Cambridgeshire

It requires a dedicated soul to don a costume that will add 30 kilograms to their weight but whoever plays lead role in the Straw Bear Festival willingly undertakes this burden. The straw bear is a 3-metre high construction of straw bundles built around a metal frame that the volunteer wears over the shoulders so that their body and head are completely obscured by dried cereal stalks.

A leash is tied around the straw bear's chest so a handler can lead it through the streets at the head of a long procession of morris, sword and clog dancers – all in costume. For about five hours the bear jigs around the town followed by an entourage of spectators and then suddenly he's gone. Even if the straw bear wanted to repeat the crowd-pleasing antics it could not – the day after the procession the costume is ritually burned in the town square. Next year the bear will return afresh born of a new harvest of straw.

Dancing, Not Begging

Plough Monday (the first Monday after Twelfth Night) traditionally marked the beginning of the new agricultural year. Farm work was scarce in winter and so farmhands – some dressed in costume – would drag a plough around the parish stopping at various points to dance and sing in exchange for money, food or beer.

In Whittlesey, from at least the nineteenth century, it was tradition for a farm labourer to disguise himself as a straw bear and be led around town with a group of friends who cheered him on as he danced. It was a make-do version of the popular real dancing bears that toured the country at that time. The local constabulary frowned upon this custom, labelling it an excuse for begging, and in 1909 it was discontinued. Revived in 1980, the January festival is a musical and dancing celebration where once again a giant moving haystack is the reason for the jollification.

Ancient Rites and Rituals

Burning of Bartle in West Witton, Yorkshire

On the Saturday nearest to St Bartholomew's feast day, 24 August, Owd Bartle meets a blazing end. Bartle is a life-sized figure made from old clothes stuffed with straw, wearing a pair of wellies, beard and hair trimmed with fleece, an ugly mask for a face and glowing eyes lit by battery-operated bulbs.

As the sun sets on the Wensleydale village of West Witton a crowd several hundred strong follows two villagers who carry Bartle on their shoulders through the settlement. They pass close by the houses, ensuring that Bartle peers through the windows, and stop outside pubs and other notable buildings as the chanter steps forward to sing Bartle's rhyme:

> On Penhill Crags he tore his rags
> At Hunters Thorn he blew his horn
> At Capplebank Stee he brak' his knee
> At Grassgill Beck he brak' his neck
> At Wadhams End he couldn't fend
> At Grassgill End we'll mak' his end
> Shout, lads, Shout!

After each rendition everyone responds with a cacophonous 'Hip hip hooray!'. It takes an hour for Bartle to complete the trek through West Witton after which he makes his final journey up to Grassgill End. Once there he is propped up against a dry-stone wall for a final performance of the rhyme. He is then doused with flammable liquid, set alight and left to burn to ashes as the crowd sings folk songs in celebration of Yorkshire.

So who was Bartle, and why such an unhappy fate? There are several theories. One of them suggests that it was a harvest celebration of corn. Bartle represents a sheaf that was ceremoniously burnt to defeat the evil corn spirit before it could destroy the harvest. Another theory proposes that Bartle was a real-life swine thief who was killed by villagers for his crimes. Or the name Bartle could be related to Baal, the Pagan god of nature and fertility. Burning of Bartle is unique to West Witton so maybe the effigy represents a folklore figure – the Penhill Giant. Penhill overlooks West Witton and the giant who lived there terrorised the villagers. He claimed to be descended from the Norse god Thor and was anything but a good neighbour. Perhaps the annual fire ritual is revenge for the fear he spread among the locals.

West Wittonites have been burning Owd Bartle for at least 400 years and next August they will be doing it once again.

A Dale Called Wensley

Wensleydale is one of few Yorkshire Dales valleys to take its name from a village (Wensley) rather than a river (the Ure). It is arguably best known for the eponymous pale crumbly cheese made in the valley since 1150 when French Cistercian monks from the Roquefort region established a monastery at Fors. The monks grazed sheep and goats on the moorland and used surplus milk to produce a distinctive cheese. It is still produced at a creamery in the dale (the town of Hawes) but is now more commonly made from cows' milk.

Randwick Wap in Randwick, Gloucestershire

Wap is a rather obscure word that may stem from the Saxon term *'wappenshaw'* translated as 'a gathering of battle-ready men'. Today, however, Randwick's most fearsome warrior is the Mop Man, who wields a wet mop to clear a pathway through the crowds as he leads the May procession. People in the parade dress up in costume – some in the garb of medieval peasants, others as eighteenth-century milkmaids.

Two principal characters, the focus of this annual tradition, are carried shoulder high through the village. The mayor, resplendent in a Restoration-era velvet frock coat, breeches, and lace collar and cuffs, and the Wap Queen – a local teenager in white frothy gown and an ornate headdress. Mr Mayor and HRH have a retinue that includes a flagman, a sword-bearer, ladies-in-waiting and princesses – also dressed up to the nines. The convoy meanders through Randwick and ends up at the Mayor's Pool where His Honour is dunked in the eponymous pond and showered with spring water.

The finale takes place at a spot called Well Leaze where official cheese-bearers offer up their cargo of two Double Gloucesters – one for the mayor and the other for the Wap Queen. They compete against each other by rolling their cheese three times down the steep incline. It breaks up on its journey and a winner is determined by counting the number of pieces of each cheese that reach the bottom of the hill.

Randwick Wap may have originated as an annual feast in the Middle Ages when the church was first built. It was always a knees-up, and so that meant plenty of drunks stumbling round the village. As was the case with many lively festivals it was frowned upon by the late Victorians and the custom ceased in 1892. The vicar revived Randwick's ancient celebration in 1972 and the Wap has been a major event in the village ever since.

Hard Cheese

How to determine if a Double Gloucester is robust enough to travel: jump on the truckle with both feet and if the rind does not break open then it is ready to go. That is how cheese merchants used to perform the test – before the advent of bubble wrap.

Cheese also features in another long-standing Randwick custom each year on the first Sunday in May. Three truckles of Double Gloucester are blessed at a church service and then parishioners are invited to roll one of them anti-clockwise around the churchyard. Their ancestors did this to ward off evil spirits but nowadays it is a game, and keeping the cheese upright is harder than it looks. Afterwards one cheese is shared out, continuing the tradition of ancestors who believed that eating it would improve fertility and ensure future generations of 'Runnickers' (the local term for a Randwick resident). The other two cheeses are kept for rolling at the Wap.

Reparations for Medieval Misdemeanours

Planting of the Penny Hedge in Whitby, Yorkshire

Whitby, a quaint maritime town with a maze of alleyways and cobbled streets, is dominated by the cliff-top ruin of St Hilda's Abbey. Early on the morning before Ascension Day few people notice two men who pick their way across the sand and seaweed in Whitby harbour towards the water's edge. They lay down a bundle of wooden stakes and start to construct a hedge that will be solid enough to withstand three tides. The hedge measures little more than 1-metre square and consists of interwoven twigs. After they finish building it a person playing the role of factotum to the abbot of St Hilda's blows a horn three times and bellows: 'Out on ye! Out on ye! Out on ye!' It means 'Shame on you!' The precise provenance of this understated custom is unknown, but according to folklore it dates from 1159 when a group of noble men were hunting in forests belonging to the abbey. They chased a wild boar into the path of a hermit who gave the beast sanctuary in a chapel. Full of rage, the hunters beat the man so violently that he later died. In his last words the hermit pardoned his attackers providing they accepted a penance to build a hedge on Ascension Eve. Each year the men and their successors were to meet the abbot's bailiff in a wood where he would cut a penny worth of sticks. The following morning the hunters were to plant them in a row at the water's edge. A horn was to be blown and the denouncement loudly proclaimed to remind them of the crime they had committed.

That's the myth. A more likely explanation for the custom is that it stems from a medieval practice called a *horngarth* – an obligation owed by tenants to the lord of the manor. *Garth* is an Anglo-Saxon term for enclosure.

Penny hedge building is practised with determination but without fanfare. No one questions why it is done and the fence builders act as though it is all in a day's work to construct a tiny willow hedge on the shoreline knowing that it will soon be swept away.

Count Dracula in Whitby

Bram Stoker had visited Whitby in 1890 and been so inspired by the setting that he chose the town as the place where his fictitious creation Count Dracula lands in England and seduces his first victim, Lucy Westenra.

Tolling the Devil's Knell in Dewsbury, Yorkshire

Bell ringing on Christmas Eve is nothing unusual but a church in Dewsbury has a unique take on the practice. The bell-ringers of All Saints' parish church congregate to toll the devil's knell. They take turns to ring the tenor bell once for every year since the birth of Jesus. This is done as a reminder to parishioners of Christ's defeat of the devil. At a rate of one stroke of the bell every two seconds the ceremony is timed perfectly so the final toll is on the dot of midnight.

A popular legend states that a fifteenth-century local landowner called Sir Thomas Soothill murdered his servant boy by throwing him in a dam. As a penance Sir Thomas donated the tenor bell to the church. Nicknamed 'Black Tom' after its benefactor the bell was rung at Christmas to remind Sir Thomas of his crime.

Why this custom began is a mystery. It was revived in 1826 and with the exception of silence during World War Two and when the bells were recast the ritual has happened ever year since.

In 2000 it took just over 66 minutes to complete the cycle but as each year passes another two seconds is added to the total time. One person volunteers to count the bell strokes to ensure that the correct number is tolled.

Shoddy Town

During the Industrial Revolution Dewsbury was at the centre of the 'shoddy' industry where old woollen clothes were ground down so the fibres could be re-spun and mixed with new wool to make heavy blankets and uniforms.

Dewsbury was included in the *Domesday Book* when its name was recorded as Deusberia and Deusberie. The name means 'fortified place by a stream'.

Superstition and Exorcism

Turning the Devil's Stone in Shebbear, Devon

Lucifer is unwelcome in Shebbear. Just to remind him of this, the villagers enact an ancient custom each year on 5 November, when all eyes focus on a monolith called the Devil's Stone underneath an oak tree outside St Michael's Church.

Bell-ringers assemble inside the church at 8 p.m. and ring out a discordant peal to challenge the Devil and any other evil spirits who may think of visiting. The message is a warning for them to avoid Shebbear. As the cacophony fades away the six ringers stream out of church and surround the stone. The vicar recites a prayer and then the ringers, armed with crowbars, get to work. Purposely making a noise by shouting excitedly, they slip the metal bars under the stone and turn it over. As it measures 2 metres by 1 metre and weighs 1 tonne, this is not an easy task but turn it they must. In village folklore failure to turn the stone each year would lead to bad luck and crop failure. Just one turn of the stone protects Shebbear for the coming twelve months.

A mystery surrounds the Devil's Stone. Geologically it is a glacial erratic (a type rock that has been carried by glacial ice) of quartz that does not match any rock formations in the region. So how did it get to Shebbear? One theory suggests that it is the remnant of a standing stone dragged from elsewhere for ritual purposes. But local tradition says that it fell from Lucifer's pocket as he passed through the village on his way to hell after he was cast out of heaven.

Devilish Devon

Devon is not the place for Lucifer. Frequent wind and rain in Northlew (a village not far from Shebbear) gave rise to a local saying: 'The devil died of cold in Northlew.'

Wassailing the Apple Trees, Somerset

To ensure a plentiful apple harvest orchards must be wassailed on Old Twelfth Night (17 January). This ancient custom, once common throughout the country, is now mainly observed in cider-making areas such as Somerset, Devon and Herefordshire. One tree, known as Apple Tree Man, is chosen to represent the orchard and during the ceremony it is feted as guardian of all the others. A happy group of wassailers gathers round Apple Tree Man to drink cider and pour some on the roots. The tips of lower twigs are dipped in cider and pieces of toast soaked in cider hung from the boughs to attract good tree spirits that come in the guise of robins. To wake the trees from winter slumber wassailers create a huge din by beating pots and pans. Finally, gunshots are fired through the top branches to drive away evil spirits that reside in the tree crown and a toast is drunk to the trees: *'Waes hael'* (Middle English for 'good health') and a rendition of the wassailing song. These songs vary from place to place but contain lines such as:

> *Wassail, wassail all round the town*
> *The zider-cup's white and the zider's brown*
> *Our zider is made vrom good apple trees*
> *And now my vine vellows we'll drink if you please.*

Wassailing has been practised for centuries in the Somerset village of Carhampton. The party starts in the Butcher's Arms and then everyone troops into the orchard for the ceremony. The wassailers return to the pub for folk songs and of course to drink more cider. After all, the fruit is said to prevent melancholy and to 'smele to an old swete apple' builds a person's strength after illness. That's why an apple a day keeps the doctor away.

Wassailing – Not Just Singing to Apple Trees

Wassailing is not just confined to orchards – it also refers to the practice of door-to-door carol singing. This dates from the Middle Ages when peasants would sing outside the properties of their wealthier neighbours:

> *Wassail! wassail! all over the town*
> *Our toast it is white and our ale it is brown*
> *Our bowl it is made of the white maple tree*
> *With the wassailing bowl, we'll drink to thee.*

They carried with them a wassail bowl that contained warm spiced ale or cider with pieces of toast floating in it. After bestowing good cheer on their 'betters' the wassailers would expect the bowl to be replenished and to be given something to eat. This was not seen as a form of begging, but as seasonal 'charity'.

Whuppity Scoorie in Lanark, Lanarkshire, Scotland

In the days running up to 1 March the children of Lanark busy themselves preparing the weapons they require to scare away evil winter spirits and hail the coming of spring. To perform this important seasonal task they use munitions no more lethal than pieces of paper screwed into balls and tied to long pieces of string.

At 5.55 p.m. some two hundred children ranging in age from three years to teens assemble at Lanark Cross, the traditional town gathering spot. As the 'wee bell' in the steeple of St Nicholas' Church begins to chime six o'clock the throng suddenly bursts into action. Any malevolent forces will undoubtedly be alarmed by the noise of dozens of boys and girls running around the church perimeter hollering and swinging the paper balls around their heads. To ensure the spirits get the message this is repeated three times. As a reward for this civic duty handfuls of coins are thrown into the air and the children try and grab the money in an old tradition called scrambling.

In the nineteenth century girls did not participate in the custom as they do now and instead of paper the boys tied their caps to bits of string and swung them round. Rather than run round the church they marched towards the village of New Lanark for a punch-up with the local lads. When stone throwing became an integral part of the event the police had to calm things down. Nowadays an accidental slap round the head with a crushed up bit of paper is as violent as it gets.

Whuppity Scoorie dates to at least 1770 and there are a couple of theories about its history. It might have been a celebration of the town curfew being extended as light spring evenings replaced dark winter nights; or it could be connected with the punishment meted out to wrongdoers who were thrashed at Lanark Cross then 'scoored' (scoured or cleansed) in the river.

Next Door's World Heritage Site

New Lanark is only a couple of kilometres away from Lanark but they are separate settlements. It is a restored eighteenth-century mill village that was awarded World Heritage status in 2001. It was built in a gorge of the river Clyde to take advantage of the fast-flowing water to power the mills. The village is a living community of 185 people who reside in houses and cottages that employees of the cotton mill lived in from 1785.

Robert Owen was a mill manager from 1800 to 1825 and he transformed life in New Lanark by introducing employee welfare. Child labour and corporal punishment was abolished. Housing was decent, schooling and evening classes were available, health care was free, and food affordable. This was nothing less than a social revolution and it took place at least a century before enlightened employers elsewhere in Britain considered such benefits for their staff.

Royal Connections

Britain's status as a constitutional monarchy means that state occasions are a unique spectacle. When it comes to official business, there is no end of ceremony and tradition in the pageantry that surrounds the monarch.

Royal Maundy

'Old soldiers never die, they just fade away,' the saying goes. Not in the case of the Queen's Body Guard of the Yeomen of the Guard, however. Britain's oldest existing military corps, created in 1485 by Henry VII at the Battle of Bosworth Field, is comprised of retired members of the armed forces to form a ceremonial bodyguard for the monarch. In a Tudor costume comprising scarlet and gold doublet, white neck ruff, knee breeches and stockings, and black patent leather shoes trimmed with red, white and blue rosettes, they invariably upstage the Queen. But that uniform is no fancy dress for wimps – combined with the ornamental weaponry of sword and partizan (a 2-metre long wooden spear with steel head and crimson and yellow tassel) the marching weight of the kit is 11 kilograms.

A New Commandment

The word Maundy is derived from the Latin *mandatum*, meaning 'command', and refers to the Gospel of St John, where Jesus says to his disciples at the Last Supper, 'A new commandment I give unto you, that you love one another.'

Yeomen of the Guard play a central role in the annual Royal Maundy ceremony on the day before Good Friday. Maundy money is a charity dole that dates back to at least 1210, when King John donated food, clothing and other gifts to the needy in Knaresborough, Yorkshire. Edward III (1327–1377) imitated the humility demonstrated by Jesus as he washed the feet of his disciples before the Last Supper, by washing the feet of the poor at a Maundy service. Succeeding monarchs continued that humble act until 1698, when William III ceased the practice.

Every year the Queen visits a different cathedral or abbey throughout the country for Royal Maundy. During the religious service of prayers, readings and choral music she hands out white and red leather purses to men and women selected by the diocese as a reward for their contribution to community life. This is where six of the Yeomen Guards step into the limelight. Each carries above his head a solid-silver, gold-plated Alms Dish. The silverware is already weighty but when the dishes are laden with purses, holding tight is a challenge. Each year the load becomes heavier because the number of recipients depends on the monarch's age. In 2006, the year the Queen celebrated her eightieth birthday, she handed out 160 purses. For weeks beforehand the guards undertake rigorous upper body training so they are strong enough to support the weight of the dishes.

The white purse contains silver Maundy coins in denominations of one, two, three and four pence specially produced by the Royal Mint in a quantity that corresponds with the age of the monarch. Those highly prized coins are legal tender, although their provenance bestows far more worth than their face value. In the red purse regular currency totalling £5.50 represents the food and clothing that formerly comprised the monarchs' dole.

Four children chosen from local schools play supporting roles in the fifty-minute service. They carry nosegays of sweet herbs – a tradition from the days when herbs were believed to ward off infection. Each child wears a white linen towel around their waist to symbolise the era when foot washing was a feature of the Maundy ceremony. Some of the linen is antique and has been used annually since 1883. Also in attendance is the choir of Chapel Royal – six adult male singers and ten boy choristers. The men wear white surplices and the boys a distinctive seventeenth-century uniform of scarlet and gold knee-length tunics with breeches and stockings. Singing at official royal ceremonies on command of the Queen is one of the principal duties of the choir and those angelic voices add great joy to the event.

State Opening of Parliament in London

If Britain has the mother of all parliaments then the State Opening of Parliament is the mother of all pageants. Surely nothing can come close to matching it. But this incredible spectacle has a practical purpose: to inaugurate the new session of Parliament and to announce the government's proposed legislation. This event normally takes place each year in November or soon after a general election. Its roots can be traced back to the sixteenth century when Henry VIII is believed to have been the first monarch to attend, although the modern form of the ceremony dates from 1852. Other parliamentary democracies have their own state opening of parliament, but none are as fantastical as Britain's version, which arguably should be renamed the State Opening of the Wardrobe.

At the centre of proceedings is the Queen. She leaves Buckingham Palace and makes her way along the ceremonial route down the Mall and through Horse Guards to the Palace of Westminster. On that short journey she is not alone. Preceding her is a horse-drawn glass carriage escorted by a Corporal of Horse and six mounted troopers from the Household Cavalry. Inside the carriage, resting on a crimson cushion, is the Imperial State Crown and the velvet and ermine trimmed Cap of Maintenance. Alongside lies the Great Sword of State. Together these priceless treasures are known as the regalia, symbols of the Queen's authority as head of state. Riding pillion, wearing braided scarlet tail coats, blue caps, white stockings and black slip-on shoes are the Queen's Barge Master and a Waterman. Their symbolic roles date back to before the reign of Queen Victoria (1837–1901) when the crown travelled by river to Westminster from the Tower of London.

The Queen is accompanied by her husband, the Duke of Edinburgh, in the Irish State Coach and a thunderous clattering ensues as four white horses draw it along the street. Perched on the carriage rear are two footmen, decked in gold and scarlet frock coats, red knee breeches, pink silk stockings, and gold-buckled shoes. The Queen, dazzlingly attired in a silk brocade gown, long white gloves and diamond diadem – an ornamental headdress that signifies sovereignty – waves to the crowds as though unaware that the world's best-dressed juggernaut follows in her wake.

Immediately behind her comes the Household Cavalry: the troopers in shiny cuirasses (breast and back armour), metal helmets trimmed with long tails of horsehair, leather jackboots, gauntlets and swords all astride black Irish draught horses. Ahead of the procession, a marching brass band comprised of the Queen's Foot Guards in bearskin helmets heralds the approach of the royal party so that members of the armed forces lining the route can stand to attention.

Meanwhile, all is ready for the Queen's arrival at the Palace of Westminster. Earlier that morning members of the Queen's Body Guard of the Yeoman of the Guard search the cellar. They check for explosives, a tradition that dates back to the Gunpowder Plot of 1605 when Guy Fawkes tried to kill King James I and the government during the State Opening of Parliament. Like most participants in this special day, the Yeoman of the Guard is in full state dress – knee-length scarlet doublet tunic worn with white muslin neck ruff, breeches with a gilt buckle at the knee, woollen stockings, black patent-leather Oxford shoes trimmed with red, white and blue ribbon rosettes, all topped off with a Tudor bonnet.

There is another age-old ritual that also purports to ensure the Queen's safety. It dates back to the reign of Charles I (1625–1649) when relations between the king and the House of Commons were abysmal. On the morning of the State Opening of Parliament a member of the government is 'held hostage' at Buckingham Palace and released only when the monarch returns home safely. No doubt the ceremonial prisoner is treated well with a cup of tea and a home-made biscuit served on the best china. Although they are deprived of most of the pomp they can hear some of the festivities: Buckingham Palace is next to Green Park where the Royal Horse Artillery fires a forty-one-gun salute to mark this important day.

As the Queen's carriage draws up to the Sovereigns' Entrance to the Palace of Westminster, two state trumpeters in gold state dress play the Royal Salute. The Lord Great Chamberlain, in scarlet robes with the gold key of office hanging from his waist, greets the Queen and escorts her to the Robing Room where she dons the crown and her Robe of State. Created in 1953 for her coronation ceremony, the robe consists of an ermine cape and a crimson velvet ermine-lined train, almost 6 metres long, decorated with gold lace and filigree. Accompanying the Queen is the Duke of Edinburgh, resplendent in the full dress uniform of an Admiral of the Fleet complete with medals and sword. Around his neck hangs the badge of the Grand Master of the Order of the British Empire, and draped over his shoulders is the collar of the Order of the Garter.

Only now can the next stage begin. Officials carrying the Cap of Maintenance, Great Sword of State, and Mace lead the Queen and her consort to the House of Lords. To show the Queen respect, the Lord Great Chamberlain and Earl Marshall walk backwards ahead of her. The House of Lords is a sea of ceremonial livery. Lords in red robes and ermine, foreign ambassadors and high commissioners – some in national dress, judges from the High Court and Court of Appeal, and Law Lords draped in rich colours and gilt trim. As the Queen enters the chamber the lights are turned up to heighten the drama and she takes her place on the throne, surrounded by members of the royal family.

Royal Palace

The Houses of Parliament or, to use its formal name, the Palace of Westminster, is a royal palace. The site had been used as a residence for the royal family starting with Edward the Confessor in the eleventh century. That was until 1512, when a fire prompted Henry VIII to move a few hundred metres up the road to Whitehall Palace (itself now replaced by the Ministry of Defence headquarters building).

Meanwhile, the Gentleman Usher of the Black Rod – an official who acts as the Queen's courier whilst she is in the Palace of Westminster – summons the Members of Parliament from the House of Commons chamber. As he approaches the door it is slammed in his face. This gesture dates back to 1642 when Charles I entered the Commons and tried to arrest five members and it symbolises the Commons' right to exclude everyone but the sovereign's messenger.

Black Rod then knocks three times on the door with his rod. The serjeant-at-arms, responsible for security in the Commons, peers through the grille to identify the caller and the door is opened. Only then may Black Rod deliver his message. He bows to the Speaker of the House saying 'Mr [or Madam] Speaker, the Queen commands this honourable house to attend Her Majesty immediately in the House of Peers.' The MPs obey this royal command – eventually – but tradition dictates that first they dawdle to show they are not awed by the monarch. They even joke and chat as they follow the prime minister and leader of the opposition into the Lords chamber to hear Her Majesty's Most Gracious Speech.

The Lord Chancellor advances towards the Queen bearing a silk bag that holds the Speech from the Throne. It is printed on goatskin vellum (as are Acts of Parliament), a centuries-old tradition. As head of state in this constitutional monarchy, the government rules in the Queen's name and drafts the speech. The Queen reads the text in a neutral tone of voice implying neither approval nor disapproval of the policies outlined and concludes by saying, 'My Lords and Members of the House of Commons, I pray that the blessing of Almighty God may rest upon your counsels.'

The ceremony concludes a little over an hour after the Queen's departure from Buckingham Palace. The House of Lords empties of dignitaries. The Queen travels home in the same glittering style she came and just in time for lunch. The hostage is released. The Crown jeweller returns to the Tower of London to replace the regalia in its display cases which were occupied, during the jewels' absence, by small cards printed with two words of quiet understatement – 'In use'. And everyone involved – human and horse – doffs the fancy dress and breathes easy until next year.

Swan-upping on the River Thames, Berkshire

Elizabeth II, by the grace of God, of the United Kingdom of Great Britain and Northern Ireland, also claims a title that few people have heard of before – Seigneur of the Swans. That magnificent designation dates from the twelfth century when the monarch bestowed swans with royal status and asserted ownership of all mute swans in England. After all, why should anyone but the monarch be entitled to tuck into such a delicacy as swan meat? Swans were so special that during the reign of Elizabeth I anyone who interfered with breeding swans, or was caught stealing their eggs, was liable to one year's imprisonment, plus a fine.

Swans and the Vintners and the Dyers

During the medieval period the monarch gave London's livery companies the right to 'a game' of swans on the river Thames. This permitted them to cull a certain number of the birds for company feasts. Today swan is off the menu, but the vintners and the dyers continue to exercise their ancient rights over the royal birds for the sake of tradition.

Today the sovereign retains rights to all swans in open water but she exercises possession only over unmarked swans on certain reaches of the river Thames and its tributaries. Since the fifteenth century that entitlement has been shared with the Worshipful Companies of the Vintners and the Dyers (livery companies of the City of London).

Each year in the third week of July a five-day pageant called Swan Upping takes place. As well as being a colourful spectacle that attracts much interest, swan-upping has a practical purpose too – that is to take a census of the swans and ensure they are healthy.

Under the command of the Queen's Swan Marker, swan-uppers travel in six wooden rowing skiffs along a 130-kilometre stretch of the Thames between Sunbury and Abingdon. The swan-uppers form three teams. One represents the Queen, and the other two act for the vintners and dyers. They wear navy or red blazers and white trousers. Fluttering from each boat is a flag marked with a swan, which identifies the craft as being engaged in official business.

On sighting a brood of cygnets the cry of 'All up!' is the signal that work is about to commence. The boats manoeuvre into position around the swans to prevent their escape and they are taken gently from the water to the riverbank. On dry land the birds are weighed and measured, then examined by the Queen's Swan Warden for signs of injury (damage from fishing lines and hooks is common) and ringed where appropriate. If the parents are unmarked they belong to the Queen, but if they have rings around their legs they are the property of either the vintners or dyers. Up until 1998 swans' beaks were checked to identify ownership. One nick cut into it meant that the swan belonged to the dyers, and two nicks classified it as property of the vintners. Healthy swans are freed and ailing creatures are taken to a nearby swan sanctuary to be cared for.

The Queen's Swan Marker has other duties apart from swan-upping. He works year-round to monitor the health of swan populations, advises boating and fishing organisations throughout the country on swan welfare, and coordinates the safe removal of swans when necessary from stretches of the river Thames that are used for rowing regattas.

Back on the Thames, as the skiffs row past Windsor Castle oars are raised and the swan-uppers stand to attention and proclaim, 'Her Majesty The Queen, Seigneur of the Swans.'

Tower of London Ceremonies

As the hectic pace of the modern capital buzzes outside the walls of Her Majesty's Royal Palace and Fortress, inside them time appears to stand still. More commonly known as the Tower of London, this imposing fortress was built by William the Conqueror in 1078 on the banks of the river Thames. The intention was to subjugate Londoners and deter foreign invaders. It may have succeeded in the beginning but today the once impregnable citadel is stormed daily by thousands of visitors who revel in the history of this World Heritage Site.

Tradition rules the Tower of London – just look at the Yeomen of the Guard dressed in their Tudor uniform of navy and scarlet-trimmed tunics and bonnets. They are royal bodyguards and their old nickname 'Beefeaters' stems from the generous rations of meat issued as a special privilege to keep them content and loyal. Those colourful characters, all retired military personnel, are involved in the Tower's oldest custom: the Ceremony of the Keys – a ritual that has been carried out each evening for over 700 years. At precisely 9.53 p.m. the Chief Yeoman Warder of the Tower, carrying a candle lantern and the Queen's keys, is accompanied by the Escort of the Key and four Yeomen Warders to lock all the gates to the Fortress. As the group approaches the Bloody Tower a sentry raises his rifle and shouts out:

> *'Halt!' The escort is halted.*
> *'Who comes there?'*
> *'The Keys,' replies the Chief Warder.*
> *'Who's Keys?'*
> *'Queen Elizabeth's Keys.'*
> *'Pass Queen Elizabeth's Keys – all's well.'*

The sentry recognises the Chief Warder as the rightful bearer of the Queen's keys and permits the group to walk on. Then a ceremonial guard presents arms as the Chief Warder raises his bonnet and proclaims 'God preserve Queen Elizabeth'. Everyone present replies 'Amen'. To conclude the ritual a trumpeter plays the 'Last Post' and by 10 p.m. the Tower is secured for the night.

The Secret Word

To enter the Tower at night one needs a password. No computerised swipe cards for access into this royal palace, thank you! Known as 'The Word' it changes every twenty-four hours and is issued to the Governor of the Tower by the Ministry of Defence. Each day at 2.50 p.m. a group of Yeoman Warders marches to the Byward Tower where the officer in charge collects The Word, which is written on a sheet of paper and carried in a leather pouch. He disseminates the code to everyone who needs to know. Unless they can remember the password, residents who return to the Tower after dark face a night outside the gates.

One of the most ancient job titles in England is Constable of the Tower of London. The constable, or boss, is an official role that dates back to the eleventh century. In those days constables helped to keep the monarch's pantry well stocked by taking goods such as wine and oysters off merchant ships on the Thames and from traders entering London by road. Every ship that sailed upstream was duty bound to unload a quota of its cargo for the constable and thus ensure protection from the Tower's guns. If that amount of swag was not sufficient they were also entitled to seize all swans swimming under London Bridge plus any horses, oxen, cattle, pigs and sheep that tumbled into the river from the bridge, or any vehicle that fell into the Tower moat.

Today few oxen fall into the Thames but the tradition of the constable's dues is marked in a costume-filled pageant. Once a year a Royal Navy ship sails upstream and moors at Tower Wharf for a special ceremony. The crew marches to the Tower, two of them carrying a wooden pole from which a barrel of rum hangs. As they approach the gates they are challenged by the Yeoman Gaoler armed with the ceremonial axe and then granted entry. Inside they are escorted to Tower Green by Yeoman Warders in scarlet and gold full state dress, and a corps of drums. When everyone is assembled the ship captain reads a script that dates from 1381:

To the Constable of the ancient Palace and Fortress of Her Majesty's Tower of London, Greetings. Whereas King Richard the second in 1381, the fourth year of his reign, granted certain fees pertaining to the Constable, be it noted that we read those this day which treat wine. The King our sovereign maketh the Constable of the Tower of London and giveth in fee yearlie forkeeping of YT:

Item: The said Constable shall have off every galley that cometh two roundlett of wyne, and of all manner of dainties, a great quantitie.

Item: The said Constable shall have off every shippe that cometh wyth wynes, two bottles, either of them containing a gallon, one before, the other after the maste.

Item: The Lieutenant shall have off every galley that cometh a roundlett of wyne and, in the absence of the Constable, off every shopp two bottles as aforesaid.

And whereas King Richard the second in the sixth year of his reign renewed these grants pertaining to the Constable, which he stated to have run from time immemorial:

Item: From every shopp laden with wyne from Bordeaux, or elsewhere, coming to the said city, one flagon from before and another from behind the maste.

Whereas I _____ am captain of Her Majesty's ship securely moored abeam of Her Majesty's good grace.'

Constable replies:

I thank you sir, for the handsome discharge of your Dues. I accept the wyne with gratitude. When we have seen it safely bestowed in the Coeur De Lyon room, let us all ascend to the Council Chamber and refresh ourselves.

The captain presents the rum (rather than wine) to the constable who graciously invites the visitors into a timber framed building called the Queen's House where the rum is polished off in true naval style.

A popular attraction at the Tower is a group of fierce-looking black birds that strut around imperiously – the famous ravens. The collective noun for ravens is 'an unkindness', and judging by the cruel appearance of their beaks it is well deserved. The story goes that if the ravens ever leave the Tower then the monarchy will fall. Just in case, the birds each have one of their wings clipped so they are unable to fly far. Whether they would want to leave is arguable as they are treated like superstars. A Yeoman Warder, the Raven Master, cares for them and they are fed daily with fresh raw meat that alternates between chicken, liver, beef and, for a treat, the occasional rabbit – fur and all. They are also partial to bird biscuits soaked in blood. Each night the ravens are coaxed into nesting sheds to protect them from nocturnal predators such as foxes. According to legend the ravens have lived there for centuries. But when John Flamsteed, astronomer to Charles II, complained that they interrupted his work, the foolhardy king ordered the birds' destruction. Charles swiftly changed his mind when he was warned of the dire future that faced him if the ravens left. Instead, he decreed that the birds should be sheltered in perpetuity.

Alas, such a fascinating story may not be true. The Tower's official historian has scoured centuries' worth of records and found no mention of ravens until the late nineteenth century. Charles Dickens had launched a craze for pet ravens with the publication in 1841 of his novel *Barnaby Rudge* featuring a talking bird called Grip. Literary master of the gothic, Edgar Allen Poe, was so inspired by Grip he wrote a celebrated poem – 'The Raven'. Perhaps London's most famous feathered creatures were originally pets owned by the Yeoman Guards. During World War Two the Tower lost its ravens when some were killed during bombing raids or died of stress. But the myth was powerful enough for the authorities to ensure that the celebrated birds were in place on 1 January 1946 when the Tower re-opened to the public. To this date the monarchy has survived, so maybe it is wise to keep the birds happy after all.

Multitaskers

Throughout its existence the Tower of London has had multiple functions: fortress, royal residence, prison and place of execution. It has housed the royal menagerie: the royal armouries, the royal wardrobe, the royal observatory, the Royal Mint and public records.

Language

The majority of Britons speak a language often referred to as the Queen's English. This suggests that it derived from aristocrats. Far from it – English is a hybrid that grew from the dialects of raiders, traders, immigrants and others who landed on these shores over the centuries. English replaced the original native Celtish tongues, yet despite overwhelming odds against them, these are still spoken in Cornwall, Wales, Isle of Man and Scotland.

Mother Tongue

To describe English as a mongrel is no insult. It belongs to a Germanic sub-branch of the Indo-European family of languages. If that means little, think of the following as ingredients in a potage that became the English tongue. The Germanic languages of Angles, Saxons and Jutes arrived with fifth-century invaders to the British Isles where the locals spoke Celtish, possibly with a smattering of Latin. Then the Vikings dropped by in the ninth century, bringing Old Norse. The Normans settled permanently in 1066, and for about 300 years Anglo-Norman (close to Old French) was the lingo for the Royal Court, law and administration. During the English Renaissance (sixteenth and seventeenth centuries) Latin and Greek words entered the vernacular. William III, from the House of Orange-Nassau in the Netherlands, brought a Dutch influence when he became king, and German was the native tongue of Hanoverian rulers of Britain. What a tasty stew. But it was to become even spicier with international trade and the expansion of the British Empire, which reached its zenith in the late nineteenth century. Countless words borrowed from approximately 145 languages – from Afrikaans (trek) to Zulu (impala) – were included in the dictionary. Here are just ten examples of common terms that originated elsewhere: alcohol, barbecue, juggernaut, magazine, pyjamas, jingo, kayak, shampoo, tattoo and zero.

English is not shy about pinching vocabulary from other languages or making up new terms. William Shakespeare was the master at that – he coined hundreds of words, many still in use today: 'arouse' used in *Henry VI, Part II*; 'moonbeam' from *A Midsummer Night's Dream*; and 'zany' in *Love's Labour's Lost* are just three examples of phrases that the Bard introduced. This willingness to expand the dictionary explains why there are more words in English than any other language, the vocabulary expanding constantly, with around 2,500 new words and revisions to each quarterly update of the *Oxford Dictionary of English*. Estimates vary but the total is thought to be more than 900,000 words – almost twice as many as its nearest rival, the Chinese dialects, which combined contain 500,000 words.

English is such a playful language. Cockney rhyming slang is a cryptic method of speaking, where rhyming phrases replace common words. For example, 'plates of meat' means feet. To make it more complicated the word that rhymes is often omitted so 'plates of meat' might be used as, 'Sit down and rest yer plates'. Cockney rhyming slang originated as a secret argot with market traders in nineteenth-century East End London. A true cockney is someone born within the sound of Bow bells, that is the bells of St Mary-le-Bow Church on Cheapside. Before noise pollution, especially from motorised traffic and aircraft, and the construction of buildings that block or absorb sound, the Bow bells could have been heard for miles around, so the true definition of a cockney is broader than just those born in the City of London.

Cockney rhyming slang is still spoken mainly by Londoners, although there are several phrases in everyday English that people use without knowing their origin. For instance:

pork pies = lies
Are you telling me porkies?

loaf of bread = head
Come on, use your loaf.

Barnet Fair = hair
Where did you get your barnet done?

tit for tat = hat
Is that a new titfer?

china plate = mate
How are you me old china?

butcher's hook = look
Let's have a butcher's.

Tod Sloan = alone
Are you on your Tod?

Jimmy Riddle = piddle (urinate)
I need a Jimmy.

treacle tart = sweetheart
Hello treacle.

rabbit and pork = talk
He would not stop rabbiting on.

Bristol City = titty (breast)
Nice pair of Bristols!

bread and honey = money
I'm a bit short of bread at the moment.

And finally,
Berkshire Hunt = c*** (no definition required!)
Don't be such a berk.

English takes the concept of 'Why have one word when you can have hundreds?' seriously when it comes to being drunk. There are at least 150 descriptive terms including: ankled, blathered, clobbered, ganted, hammered, lashed, mullered, pickled, ratted, sloshed, trollied and wellied, for example. And when it comes to swear words or terms of mild abuse it is peerless: plonker, ninny, twit, git, nerd, wally, juggins, nincompoop, prat, chump, nitwit, dork, numpty, pranny, silly-billy and muggings, to name but a few.

Ninety-eight per cent of native-born Britons speak with a regional accent and the other two per cent with Received Pronunciation (or RP). Sometimes called the Queen's English, or BBC English, this accent reveals nothing about a person's geographical provenance but discloses a great deal about the speaker's social background, invariably categorising them as middle class and usually educated in private schools. Amongst the multitude of accents are: Estuary English (people who live along the river Thames corridor speak EE), Scouse (Liverpool), Geordie (Newcastle and Tyneside), Brummie (Birmingham), as well as dozens of others that do not have a nickname. There are also a number of dialects sprinkled with localised vocabulary – these include Cumbrian, Northumbrian, East Anglian and Mackem (Wearside). Several terms from the Yorkshire dialect have escaped from God's Own County and have passed into vernacular English. This is a brief glossary of Yorkshire:

abide = bear
I can't abide that bloke.

allus = always
Yer allus going to remember that.

apeth = a halfpenny worth
Yer daft apeth.

baht = without
Don't go baht yer coit (coat).

blether = talk nonsense
She's was blethering on about summert and nowt
(something and nothing).

bray = beat up
That lad got brayed outside t' pub.

cake'ole = mouth
Shut tha cake'ole will yer.

chuffed = pleased with oneself
I were right chuffed.

chunter = mutter
He were chuntering away to himself.

eyup = hello

gawpin' = staring
I were so embarrassed wi' everyone gawpin' at me.

keks = trousers
Do you want me wash them keks?

laiking = playing
Are you coming out laiking?

lug = ear
Have you seen t' size of his lugs?

mardy = miserable, in a bad mood
She came over all mardy.

maungy = spoilt, peevish
That brat's a right maungy little so and so.

narked = annoyed
He didn't turn up on time and I were right narked.

think on = remember
Now think on what I told yer.

Over the border from Yorkshire in Lancashire, Lanky Talk (or Twang) is full of wit, pith and wisdom. If Confucius had lived in Coronation Street his philosophical advice would surely have been along the lines of:

Th'arl come to thi cake an' milk.
You will come to your cake and milk.
(You will receive what is due.)

Beauty's only skin deep – but it's a bugger when tha 'ast use a pick ter ger at it.
Beauty is only skin deep – but it's a bugger when you need to use a pick to get at it.
(Used to describe someone as ugly.)

Muck midden pride – a carriage weddin' an' a wheelbarrow flittin'.
Muck midden [a domestic waste dump] pride – a carriage wedding and a wheelbarrow flitting [leaving stealthily, usually in debt].
(Showiness comes to nothing.)

Tha met bi born but th'art not dee-erd yet.
You might be born, but you're not dead yet.
(Don't be too complacent because bad things can happen.)

A shut meawth keeps flies eawt.
A closed mouth keeps flies out.

(Don't gossip.)

Second 'un sits on t' best knee.
The second one sits on the best knee.
(The second wife often gets better treatment than the first.)

Scottish accents are often impenetrable, even to Scots.
Here are a few idioms (with translation) to practise:

Dinna droon the miller.
Don't drown the miller.
(Don't put too much water in the whisky.)

Twa bubbles aff the centre.
Two bubbles off the centre.
(Used to describe someone a bit stupid – derived from the bubbles in a spirit level.)

Mak a kirk or a mill o' it.
Make a church or a mill of it.
(It's your choice.)

He's goat mair degrees than a thermometer.
He has got more degrees than a thermometer.
(Used to describe someone very clever.)

A tongue that would clip clouts.
A tongue that would cut clothes.
(Used to describe someone who is sharp tongued.)

Auld claes and cauld porritch.
Old clothes and cold porridge.
(Out of money.)

LANGUAGE

Haud up yer heid like a thistle.
Hold up your head like a thistle.
(Be a proud Scot.)

Celtic Tongues

English is not the only native tongue heard in these isles. Welsh, Cornish, Scottish Gaelic, and Manx Gaelic in the Isle of Man (the island is within British territorial waters but is not a part of the United Kingdom) are spoken by people keen to retain their Celtic heritage.

Long before the English language existed and before the Latin-speaking Romans landed in AD 43 and colonised the island for almost 400 years, inhabitants of Britain – the Celts – spoke variations of Celtish. From AD 410 successive hostile invasions from northern Europe pushed Celts westward to what is now Cornwall and Wales, where the language survived. Meanwhile in Scotland, the Scotti (from Ireland) and Picts – both Celtish speaking peoples – ensured that the language did not die out. Welsh and Cornish belong to a branch of Celtish called Brythonic, whereas Scottish Gaelic and Manx are from a strand of Celtish known as Goidelic. Although both have a percentage of common vocabulary, Cornish and Welsh are more closely related, just as Scottish and Manx Gaelic are. In theory, speakers of those languages should be able to understand each other. Modern Britain has very few monoglot Celtish speakers.

Welsh is the most widely spoken Celtic tongue. According to the latest government census (2001) more than one fifth of the population of Wales can speak it. A substantial proportion of those people live in the west and north-west of the land. Walk into a shop in the town of Llanberis, for instance, and chances are the staff will be chatting in Welsh – then out of politeness they normally switch to English if the customer is not local. A number of primary schools educate pupils exclusively in Welsh but these children will learn English too because they need to be bilingual. Television (S4C) and radio (Cymru) broadcast in Welsh and ensure that it is a dynamic and living language.

LANGUAGE

The Welsh alphabet differs from its English counterpart in several ways. There is no 'K' 'Q' 'V' 'X' or 'Z'. 'Y' is a vowel and there are double consonants. This is how it reads:

A B C CH D DD E F FF G NG H I J L LL M N O P PH R RH S T TH U W Y

So without Z or Q, how can a top score in Scrabble be achieved? The answer is to play with the official Welsh language version launched in 2005. High value letters are NG or RH – they appear together on one tile and are worth ten points, whereas common-or-garden DD only merits one point.

Place names beginning with 'Ll' are widespread throughout Wales. Arguably the best known is: Llanfairpwllgwyngyllgogerychwyrndrobwllllantysiliogogogoch on the island of Anglesey. This is the lengthiest name of a settlement in Britain and it also holds the world record for being the longest registered website domain name of one word without hyphens. Translated into English the moniker means 'St Mary's church in the hollow of the white hazel near to the rapid whirlpool and the church of St Tysilio of the red cave'. Residents in a verbal hurry refer to their village with condensed versions – Llanfair, Llanfair PG or Llanfairpwll.

English speakers struggling to find a user name not already taken by those countless people who use the Internet auction site eBay might want to look to Wales, where the place names are a gold mine for out-of-the-ordinary spellings. Cwm y Glo, a hamlet in Snowdonia, though already taken is a prime example. Emails from eBay that start off 'Dear Cwm y Glo' raise a chortle each time.

Names of Welsh settlements are so much more descriptive than their English counterparts. Here are five notable sounding places to consider visiting in Wales: Nant y Bustach – translates as the bullock's glen; Pantysgallog - translates as valley of the thistles; Chwilog – translates as land infested with beetles; Bryn Bwbach– translates as goblin hill; Craig y Cythraul – translates as the Devil's rock.

For centuries Cornish was spoken by virtually everyone in Cornwall – 95 per cent in 1050. By 1700 that figure was reduced to five per cent as English became the dominant language. There are conflicting opinions about whether the last native speaker was Dolly Pentreath who died in 1777, or Alison Treganning who passed away in 1906. The Cornish language (*Kernewek*) is undergoing a renaissance and although there are currently only a few hundred people who are fluent, thousands of enthusiasts speak some Cornish and are keen to sustain the county's original tongue. The British Government recently recognised Cornish under the European Charter for Regional or Minority Languages. It is now taught in certain schools, councils are erecting bilingual signs, and language buffs meet in the pub to hone their skills. A typical Cornish conversation might begin:

Dydh da. (Good day.) *Ass yw brav an gewer.* (What fine weather.) *Fatla genes?* (How are you?)

Yn point da meur ras.
(I am well thank you.)

Pandra vynn'ta dh'y eva?
(What do you want to drink?)

Pinta korev marpleg.
(A pint of beer please.)

Yeghes da/Sewena!
(Cheers!)

LANGUAGE

Visitors to Scotland may be familiar with the Gaelic greeting, *'Ceud mìle fàilte!'* – in English it means 'one hundred thousand welcomes'. Statistics from the government census in 2001 reveal that just over one per cent of the population speaks Scottish Gaelic. A majority of those are based in the Western Isles where 61 per cent claim to use it. Since the passing. in 2005, of the Gaelic Language (Scotland) Act, more schools are teaching it and radio and TV channels broadcast some Gaelic programmes. Several anglicised Gaelic words have been subsumed by the English lexicon. 'Whisky' is a corruption of *uisge beatha* (pronounced ishka ba-ha) – itself a translation of the Latin *aqua vitae* or 'water of life'. Other borrowed words include: brogue (Gaelic *bròg* meaning shoe), glen (*glean* meaning valley), clan (*clann* meaning family), slogan (*sluagh-ghairm* meaning battle cry), trousers (*triubhas),* pillion (*pillean* meaning pack saddle), hubbub (*ubub* being an exclamation of disapproval), smidgen (*smidean* meaning a small bit*).*

In the Isle of Man (or *Ellan Vannin,* in Manx), an island situated in the Irish Sea between Northern Ireland and mainland Britain, the original native tongue, Manx Gaelic (*Y Ghailck*), is descended from Old Irish. A revival has been under way since the mid-twentieth century with schools now teaching Manx as a second language and several families choosing to speak it at home. New laws passed through the island's parliament, the Tynwald, are proclaimed in both Manx and English by an official called *Yn Lhaihder* (the Reader) out in the open on Tynwald Hill each year on 5 July.

If William Shakespeare had been a Manx man, Richard III's anguished cry during the Battle of Bosworth Field would have read: *'Cabbyl, cabbyl, my reeriaght son cabbyl!* ('A horse, a horse, my kingdom for a horse!') Hours could be spent on Manx language websites discovering gems such as *Caillin y Saveen Liauyr* for Sleeping Beauty, a taxidermist is *pronneyder sheh,* and *'Daa phynt dy lhune freillagh as poagey dy vrishlagyn, my saill'* which means, 'Two pints of lager and a packet of crisps, please.' Very handy to know for anyone embarking on a *turrys iu* (pub crawl). Just don't fall in a *fank* (sheep pen) on the way home.

Ulster Scots

Ulster Scots is spoken in Northern Ireland by a minority of the community (the total is believed to range between 30,000 and 100,000 people). It is not a Celtic language, rather a variation of Scots that arrived with Scottish immigrants during the seventeenth century. Over the years it has been influenced by Mid Ulster English (the local dialect) and Irish Gaelic. For instance: 'Hello. Are you well?' would be '*Hi ye daen. Ir ye weel?*' Ulster Scots is sometimes called Ullans, a neologism that merges 'Ulster' and 'Lallans' – the Scots word for 'lowlands'. Scots began in the seventh century as a regional variant of the Northumbrian dialect of Anglo Saxon, and incorporated Middle English from the fourteenth century.

Great British Grub

Ask a visitor from overseas to name a traditional British meal and chances are they will suggest roast beef or fish and chips. They are unlikely to mention fidget pie or lobscouse unless they have eaten their way around Britain and tasted some of the regional dishes. Tasty though they are, some of those local delicacies are not just confined to the plate.

Food Fights and Contests

World Black Pudding Throwing Championships in Ramsbottom, Lancashire

Incessant battles between the Houses of York and Lancaster during the fifteenth century became known as the Wars of the Roses. Ostensibly, the Yorkists came out on top when Henry Tudor became King Henry VII. But there was no real end to hostilities because Yorkshire and Lancashire have been fighting a low-level conflict ever since through cricket and other sports, not least the World Black Pudding Throwing Championships. On the surface this may seem to be harmless fun, but look a little closer. Black pudding is a typical Lancashire dish and during the competition those dark sausage-shaped missiles are hurled towards a pile of innocent Yorkshire puddings, culinary symbol of the white rose county. Warfare by proxy.

Each September several hundred combatants travel to the Pennines town of Ramsbottom for a chance to be victor in the World Black Pudding Throwing Championships. It has global appeal attracting entrants from Europe, Africa, the Americas and the Antipodes. In the days before there is much preparation. A few hundred black puddings are swaddled in nylon (filched from ladies' pantyhose) to prevent tampering. Just as cricketers gain advantage from interfering with the ball, so might pudding-chuckers. The synthetic covering also protects the missiles from falling to pieces when they thud on the ground after a throw. The puddings are made to a specific competition weight of 170 grams – the optimum load for a successful lob.

A scrumptiousness (that's the unofficial collective noun) of round Yorkshire puddings is purchased. In wet weather they go from crispy to soggy and that makes them harder to knock over, so the targets need to be replaced frequently to ensure each player has an equal chance. And talking of equality... Yorkshire pudding is a perfect blend of milk, flour and eggs baked in an oven. Made properly it can be as light as an angel's breath. Can something that weighs so little possibly compete on equal terms with the pugnacious pork blood sausage?

Before the championship can commence the golden grid – a piece of metal that marks where players stand and throw – is carried to Ramsbottom aboard a steam train. Scottish bagpipes herald its arrival and it is ceremoniously borne through town to the Royal Oak. Projectiles are in place. Yorkshire puddings are piled up on the exterior ledge of the pub wall. The crowd swells in anticipation. Let the games begin.

Competitors stand on the golden grid and take aim. They can throw using any technique they choose – as long as it is under-arm. The lob is consistently effective and a popular manoeuvre for seasoned entrants. It requires concentration and the confidence to add a little spin so the weapon decimates the mounds of Yorkshires.

With hundreds of people participating in the competition it can be hours before the winner is declared. To keep everyone amused there are other diversions such as a separate pudding throwing competition for children and Pudstock, an open-air music festival featuring local bands.

When scores are finally tallied the junior and adult winners are declared and the two expert pitchers crowned world champions. Just like Olympic medallists, the triumphant black pudding flingers will forever be in an exclusive club.

Global Grub

Local versions of black pudding or blood sausage are eaten in most parts of the world – *morcilla* in Spain, *boudin noir* in France, and *Blutwurst* in Germany. In the UK, where black pudding's spiritual home is Lancashire, it is made from a blend of pig blood, pork fat and cereal (oatmeal or barley).

Yorkshire pudding, on the other hand, has no aliases. Alongside roast beef it is shorthand for down-to-earth English cuisine. In many Yorkshire homes people still eat it before the main course – a hangover from the days when it was used to fill up those who could not afford much meat. Despite being a simple dish of milk, eggs and flour there is an art to making it. The trick is to get the fat dangerously hot in the pudding tin before pouring in the batter. Heat the fat using the gas ring of a cooker until it smokes. Pour in the mixture and let it cook for a while, *then* stick it in the oven. Never fails.

Cheese Rolling in Brockworth, Gloucestershire, and Stilton, Cambridgeshire

Cooper's Hill is anything but a gentle incline. In some parts the gradient is one in one. Each Spring Bank Holiday dozens of people hurl themselves down the precipice in pursuit of a 3.5-kilogram truckle of Double Gloucester cheese. But this is no ordinary *fromage* – it is the only such cheese in the county still made by hand from the milk of Brown Swiss, Holstein and Gloucester cows. So it's worth breaking a bone for. Or getting concussion. Certainly bruising. Yet despite the ambulance being on speed-dial, this fiesta is so popular the organisers are inundated with entries.

Days before the event the hill surface is cleared of nettles and brambles and a crash barrier of straw bales is erected. There's no question that it will be needed as the racers hurtle down an almost vertical cliff chasing a cheese that rolls at a speed of 100 kilometres per hour.

For some competitors, race day is the first time they have seen the hill in real life. As fear gnaws their stomach the temptation to drop out is overwhelming, but saving face in front of several thousand spectators is a strong motivator. At the start of each race a line-up of 20 entrants stands on the flat summit. There is no going back as the master of ceremonies, dressed in the white coat of a cheese-maker and wearing a top hat trimmed with ribbons, announces: 'One to be ready. Two to be steady. Three to prepare. And four to be off!' Simultaneously, the cheese is released and disappears into the abyss. Racers hurl themselves after it but there is no chance of staying upright and most people bounce violently down the 230-metre course, tumbling every which way. A winning time is around 12 seconds – the first to the bottom wins the cheese and the satisfaction of completing a race that makes a black diamond ski run seem like a nursery slope in comparison.

Few escape being cut and bruised in the execution of the contest. Some do not even finish the course and those unlucky enough to sustain a serious injury are carried off Cooper's Hill by a search and rescue team using specialist mountain recovery equipment.

Cheese rolling in Brockworth dates at least to the early nineteenth century but it is unclear when or why it started. In the modern era the competition has been cancelled only three times, although the organisers still privately rolled a cheese down the hill so they could claim an unbroken heritage. During World War Two, food rationing should have stymied the event but Brockworthians are determined folks and continued their unique sport by fashioning a wooden replica truckle with a hole that contained the tiniest piece of real cheese. To use that morsel they required permission from the Ministry of Food. The competition returned with a delicious full-sized Double Gloucester in 1954 when rationing was abolished.

A more genteel version of cheese rolling takes place in the village of Stilton on May Day bank holiday. Teams, often in fancy dress, compete to roll a wooden replica of the eponymous cheese down the streets. It is a knockout contest and the victors win a whole (real) Stilton and a supply of beer or wine.

Although the celebrated blue cheese shares a name with the Cambridgeshire village, it was never actually made there. The connection arose because of Stilton's location on a north–south coaching route. A cheese maker from Melton Mowbray in Leicestershire took her wares to Stilton's Bell Inn and travellers had the opportunity to taste and buy the mouth-watering delicacy. As early as 1727, author Daniel Defoe mentioned in his writings, *A Tour Through the Whole Island of Great Britain*, that Stilton was famous for its cheese.

The strategic importance of Stilton village waned as railways replaced horse-driven coaches. In the early 1960s the landlords of The Talbot Inn and The Bell Inn Hotel concocted an annual event that might lure visitors. And lo the ancient sport of cheese rolling was born.

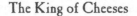

The King of Cheeses

To be labelled as Stilton, 'the King of Cheeses' must be made with local milk from one of only six dairies located in Derbyshire, Leicestershire and Nottinghamshire. The distinctive blue veins are *Penicillium roqueforti* mould spores.

World Nettle Eating Championships in Marshwood, Dorset

Athletes talk of 'feeling the burn' when they push themselves to the limits of their sport. How would they cope with feeling the sting? That is the obstacle facing competitors in the World Nettle Eating Championships. Each year in June vanloads of nettles are delivered to the Bottle Inn to feed the appetite of contestants who turn up ready for the challenge of spending one hour consuming and keeping down more nettles than anyone else. Some tender-tongued folk might classify this as an extreme sport due to the nettles' weapon – spiny hairs on the top-side of the leaves that, when touched, infuse the skin with a cocktail of poisons.

The Bottle Inn beer garden is packed with spectators as contenders sit down for a feast. On each table bunches of raw nettles chopped into 60-centimetre-long stems are piled up. As with asparagus, nettles can be picked up with the fingers for consumption. The trick is to grasp the nettles firmly rather than brushing against the leaves; that way the hairs are crushed down flat and do not penetrate the skin so easily.

Nettle eating is a freestyle contest so there are a number of techniques. Neophytes daintily chew the leaf but real contenders will swiftly strip the leaves off, making sure to avoid the sting by handling the underside, then stuff them in the mouth, chew, swallow and repeat – again and again. It's quite likely the mouth will become numb and even swollen. No deadening agents are permitted, although gulps of ale between mouthfuls are advised. If, as the saying goes, a week is a long time in politics, then an hour chomping nettles is an age.

Marshwood's eating contest originated in 1989 following an argument between two farmers about who had the longest nettle on their land. The Bottle Inn landlady suggested an open competition to see who could find the biggest specimen. One local brought in a monster that measured 5 metres and proclaimed that he would eat it if anyone found one that was longer. True to his word, when an even lengthier plant was discovered the vanquished collector sat in a corner of the beer garden and started nibbling. That solo effort inspired the world championship. Compared to current record holders 5 metres is a mere appetiser – a former champion managed to eat the leaves off so many nettle stems that when stuck together they measured 25 metres.

Cooking renders the stinging hairs harmless and neutralises poisons. Cooked nettle leaves have a flavour similar to spinach and are rich in vitamins A, C and D, iron, potassium, manganese and calcium. Freegans and hedgerow hunter-gatherers may already regularly tuck into nettle soup. For those who have never tasted that delicious potage it is easy to make. Just don't forget to wear gloves for the harvest. Choose only the younger bright green leaves and pick enough to fill a carrier bag. Chop them into a pan with a litre of stock, two medium onions, two medium potatoes, 250 millilitres of milk, seasoning and a knob of butter. Blend after cooking, then serve.

To Grasp the Nettle

After a long day of marching, Roman soldiers would pick stinging plants to beat each other's aching body parts with. The practice is known as urtication and it means 'a lashing with nettles' – a procedure that can be used to stimulate the skin, treat paralysis, or as a remedy for rheumatism. Just don't mention urtication to anyone at the Bottle Inn – eating nettles raw is painful enough.

Regional Repasts

Chances are that Sunday dinner in a British house today means a roast chicken. Spare a thought for the wild birds of Britain in the medieval era when it was common to eat lark, curlew, song thrush, swan, peacock, fieldfare, blackbird, plover, crane, teal – all at one sitting. That was in addition to regular game birds – partridge, pheasant and woodcock. Never mind the rabbit, venison, boar and oxen. All meat and no two veg. In those days feasting and conspicuous consumption equalled power: to the wealthy, food was not just sustenance; it also demonstrated status. Hospitality was extravagant and tables laden with lavish victuals were a way to impress, to reward and to do business. Abundance was a sign of success. But for the majority of Britons, food was basic and there was less of it. Anything foraged or inexpensive would end up in the pot and leftovers were transformed into new dishes. Nothing was wasted – that joke about the squeal being the only unused part of the pig was true.

Today, peacocks decorate the garden rather than the dinner table and across Britain simpler grub such as toad-in-the-hole and bangers and mash is eaten by rich and poor alike. There are a number of dishes consumed in specific areas and nowhere else, so it is possible to eat one's way through the country tasting regional delicacies. Some of them are easy to find in shops and in restaurants, others might just be cooked in private kitchens – in which case angling for an invitation home might be the only way to sample them.

The selection of foods below has been included for a variety of reasons – for their great significance to the community, because they are available only in a specific region, for their marvellous names, or because there is something unusual or poignant about them.

England

Bedfordshire

Cattern (sometimes spelled kattern) Cakes, also known as Catherine cakes were traditionally eaten in Bedfordshire on St Catherine's Day, 25 November. They are sweet doughy buns spiced with caraway seeds. St Catherine was the patron saint of lacemakers and many people in the county depended on lace for their livelihood. According to legend, Catherine of Aragon, who lived at Ampthill Castle during her divorce from Henry VIII, burned her lace so she would need to order anew, thereby giving work to local lacemakers.

Bedfordshire clangers form a complete meal, with a savoury filling such as seasoned pork at one end of the suet pastry shell and fruit at the other. Like its cousin the Cornish pasty, it was originally a practical method for labourers to carry their lunch with them. The name may come from a dialect word 'clang', meaning to eat voraciously.

Berkshire

Windsor may be best known for its royal castle, but less grand is a simple dessert called poor knights of Windsor. It is slices of bread fried in a mixture of wine, milk, and sugar, eaten with jam. Originally, the Poor Knights of Windsor was an organisation formed by King Edward III in the fourteenth century to provide assistance for retired soldiers in penury.

Across the river from Windsor sits the town of Eton, location of the eponymous private school where a dessert called Eton mess originated around the 1930s. It consists of pieces of meringue, whipped cream and strawberries messily stirred up together.

Cornwall

Cornwall introduced the world to the Cornish pasty – a hand-held hearty lunch that tin miners took to work. The traditional filling consists of seasoned meat, potato and swede, but there are no rules and so anything goes. Pasties date at least to the Middle Ages and over the years folklore has grown around the iconic delicacy. Superstitious miners would save a pastry corner to leave for the Knockers – mythical 'little people' who created monkey business in the mines. A little snack would placate the mischievous creatures and might even bring good luck to the miner. And a local legend claims that the Devil would be too scared to cross the river Tamar from Devon into Cornwall in case he ended up as an ingredient in a pasty.

A lesser-known Cornish delicacy is stargazey pie (also known as starry gazey pie), made with pilchards and hard-boiled eggs. The unusual name refers to the fish heads that stick out of the pastry so that they gaze up to the sky. This dish commemorates the bravery of Tom Bawcock, a sixteenth-century fisherman from Mousehole who saved the villagers from starvation when a sustained period of stormy weather had prevented the fishing boats from being launched. Tom rowed into the heavy ocean swell, cast his nets and returned later with a significant haul of fish. According to the legend he was presented with a Stargazey Pie in gratitude for his heroism. Each year on 23 December, residents of Mousehole celebrate Tom Bawcock's Eve with a parade of home-made paper lanterns in the shape of fish, boats and of course the famous pie. A piper and drummer lead the procession down to the beach where a choir sings carols as the lanterns are floated out to sea. Afterwards the place to be is The Ship Inn when a specially made stargazey pie is unveiled for all to eat.

Cumbria

Cumbria (formerly Cumberland and Westmoreland) has long been celebrated for its dairy produce. Cumberland rum butter contains unsalted butter flavoured with rum, brown sugar and spices. It was traditionally served to celebrate the birth of a baby and coins were stuck to the buttery remains around the bowl to ensure a happy life for the newborn.

England/Welsh Border Counties

Fidget pies, also called fitchett pies, were once widely eaten in the Midlands and Welsh border counties. Ingredients varied depending on what was seasonally available – bacon, onions and apples were common – and the pies were portable so working men could take them for lunch. The name may be a corruption of 'fitched', meaning five-sided – referring to the pie's distinctive, original shape. Local versions are still made today in Shropshire, Herefordshire and Cheshire.

Kent

Kent Lent pie, also known as Kentish pudding pie, combines milk, butter, sugar, eggs, currants and lemon rind in a dessert that resembles a cheesecake.

Until the Reformation in the sixteenth century Lent was strictly observed and anything tasty was prohibited. Diets of the faithful could be rather monotonous so this pie was a treat eaten just before the period of abstinence began. It would also have been a way to use up ingredients that were forbidden during the Lenten season.

Lancashire

Lancashire has a love affair with the potato – it forms the basis of the famous hot pot and also a dish called lobscouse. This is a stew of potato, onion and seasoning with a small amount of meat. It was especially popular in Liverpool and is the reason that Liverpudlians are nicknamed 'scousers'.

Sad cakes are eaten in Rossendale and are a variation of the county's better-known Eccles and Chorley cakes – dried fruit in puff pastry. The name may be a jocular reference to the fact that the cake is flat and rather humble.

London

London Particular is a green split-pea soup devised in the nineteenth century by a chef at Simpson's-in-the-Strand restaurant. It took its name from the infamous smogs, also known as pea-soupers, which blanketed the capital until the Clean Air Act 1956 outlawed the burning of soft coal.

Another London soup with the rather unappetising name of water souchet is made with fish leftovers. Its name likely originated from a Dutch fish dish called *waterzootje*.

North-east England

North-east England has a number of wonderfully named savoury and sweet dishes. Pan haggerty consists of sliced potato, onions and grated cheese cooked together with oil or butter then grilled to brown the top. It should always be served directly from the pan in which it is cooked.

Whitley goose might disappoint carnivores expecting succulent fowl – it is a mixture of boiled onions, cheese and milk baked in an oven. The dish originated in the town of Whitley Bay and the name is most likely a joke about the modest ingredients.

Bacon floddie is a fried hash of onion, bacon, potato and flour usually served with a breakfast fry-up. It is a traditional dish in the Tyneside town of Gateshead.

Hinny is a term of endearment in the north-east, and singing hinnies are fruit teacake-style griddlecakes that sing and sizzle during cooking.

Mouth-watering layers of sponge liberally spread with thick whipped cream and fresh strawberries are known as courting cakes and were traditionally made by newly betrothed girls to impress their fiancés.

The fat rascal is a round domed teacake with a rich brown crust made with currants and candied peel.
Lindisfarne is renowned for its mead (fermented honey and water) used in a creamy dessert called Holy Island syllabub.

Oxfordshire

Hollygog pudding is a syrup and butter dessert baked into a roll, cut into slices and served with custard or cream.

Somerset

Somerset bath chaps are smoked pig's cheek boiled and often coated with golden breadcrumbs then fried. They can be served hot or cold.

Surrey

Maids of honour are curd cheese tarts eaten as a dessert. The story goes that Henry VIII named them after he saw Anne Boleyn and her entourage eating the tartlets. The king was a glutton and according to the legend he wanted to keep the recipe all for himself and so it was locked away in an iron box at Richmond Palace.

Warwickshire

Coventry godcakes are made with spicy fruit mincemeat and puff pastry. In the past godparents gave them to their godchildren for good luck. Their triangular shape represents the Holy Trinity, hence the name.

A speciality of Warwickshire is plum jerkum or jercum – a country cider made with plums instead of apples.

Wiltshire

Wiltshire lardy cake lives up to its name – bread dough folded with lard, sugar and dried fruit then baked until crisp and brown. Another dessert from the same county is Wiltshire fairings – they resemble flat brandy snaps made of syrup, sugar, butter and flavoured with spices.

Yorkshire

Think Yorkshire, think pudding. But which one? There is an alternative to the ubiquitous variety made from flour, milk and egg. What about dock pudding, made with *Polygonum bistorta*, the sweet dock leaf? It is such a delicacy in the white rose county that the Pennines village of Mytholmroyd hosts the World Dock Pudding Championships each year in April. Entrants boil up a combination of dock leaves, nettle tops, oatmeal and onions. The following day, in front of spectators at the local leisure centre, competitors fry dollops of their own mixture and serve it with bacon and eggs. A panel of four adjudicators taste the entries and judge them for flavour, texture and presentation. The prize is a trophy, and of course the accolade of being the world's best.

Another Yorkshire village with a world-beating signature dish is Denby Dale. In a tradition dating from 1788 villagers create huge meat pies to celebrate national events. In this case huge means gargantuan – the most recent pie, baked to celebrate the Millennium, measured 13 metres long, 3 metres wide, 1 metre deep and weighed 12 tonnes. It entered the *Guinness World Records* book as the largest pie ever baked. A specially constructed dish was divided into twenty-four compartments each heated by an individual element. On Pie Day the giant savoury was transported on a wagon in a parade led by a brass band and followed by majorettes, shire horses, and stilt walkers. The Bishop of Wakefield blessed the record breaker before it was cut up and distributed.

The first Denby Dale pie was baked to celebrate the return to health of King George III. Since then the feat has been repeated nine times to commemorate significant events including victory at the Battle of Waterloo, repeal of the corn laws and Queen Victoria's Golden Jubilee.

Scotland

Scotland arguably has the most inventive names for its regional dishes:

Skirlie, also known as mealie jimmy, is a type of stuffing that consists of dripping, onions, oatmeal and seasonings all skirled (fried) together in a pan.

Cullen skink is finnan haddie (smoked haddock) and potato soup that originated in the fishing village of Cullen in Morayshire. Skink is a Scots word that means 'shin' but that came to refer to 'soup' because the basis of a hearty Scottish potage was usually shin beef.

Crappit heids comprises the heads of large fish such as cod, cleaned and stuffed with fish liver and oatmeal. This dish originated in northern Scotland fishing communities when valuable filets of fish were sold at market and the cheaper cuts, the heads and offal, were kept for the fishermen to eat. It made an inexpensive and nutritious meal.

Clapshot originated in the Orkney Islands and is often eaten as an accompaniment to haggis. It is a combination of potato and turnip/swede mashed with chives.

Like London, Scotland's capital city was once plagued by intense smog and earned itself the nickname 'Auld Reekie' (Old Smoky). Edinburgh fog is a rich, thick dessert made with double cream, almonds, sugar, and flavoured with whisky.

Howtowdie is braised chicken normally served on a bed of creamed spinach topped with drappit (poached) eggs. The name may come from the Old French word *hutaudeau* meaning a pullet.

Parton bree is crab soup. The name is derived from the Gaelic word for crab – *parton*.

Feather fowlie is chicken and vegetable soup.

Rumbledethumps is a combination of potato, vegetables and butter rumbled (mixed) and thumped (mashed together). It is eaten on its own or as an accompaniment to stews or roasts.

Tweed kettle is fresh salmon, white wine and herbs in a light stew. It is often served with bashed neaps or tatties (mashed turnips or potatoes). The river Tweed is one of Scotland's great salmon fishing rivers.

Whim wham is a sherry trifle that originated in the eighteenth century when the term whim-wham was used to describe something light and fanciful.

Wales

Welsh rarebit is widely eaten both in and outside Britain. But it could be argued that Cawl is the national dish of Wales. Recipes vary depending on region and personal taste but originally Cawl would have included scraps of meat, leeks and cabbage cooked together in a stewing pot over a fire. Cawl can be eaten all together in a bowl, although in some houses the broth is served first and the meat and vegetables make up a second course.

Anglesey eggs (*wyau ynys môn*) is a meal of eggs in cheese sauce with creamy potatoes and leeks, grilled until crisp on top. This dish is a simple way to use up leftovers.

Laver bread, or *bara lawr* in Welsh, is typically served as a breakfast dish. Despite it being called bread, it would not be found in a bakery. Laver is edible seaweed that grows along the coast of Wales. For eating, it must be washed several times to remove sand then boiled for a few hours. Chop it up then mix with oatmeal to form patties and fry them until crisp on both sides, preferably in bacon fat.

Bara brith, or to use the less tasty English translation, 'speckled bread', can confidently claim to be Wales' national fruitcake. Perfect eaten fresh from the oven, or toasted and spread with Welsh salted butter, this cake is widely available in shops, bakeries and tearooms. Serious bakers of bara brith will soak the dried fruit overnight in strong tea and the following day add the remaining ingredients – marmalade, egg, flour, brown sugar and spice.

Northern Ireland

Champ is a popular dish made of potatoes chunkily mashed with chopped spring onions, milk, butter and seasoning.

Boxty, once a traditional Halloween dish, now eaten year round consists of cooked and raw (grated) potato, flour and sugar made into dough then cooked on a griddle. Add milk to the mixture and it can be fried as a pancake and eaten with brown sugar and butter. According to the old rhyme, women should eat boxty if they want a husband.

> Boxty on the griddle, boxty in the pan
> The wee one in the middle is for Mary Ann
> Boxty on the griddle, boxty in the pan,
> If you don't eat boxty, you'll never get your man.

Return of the Natives

Historically, the economies of Whitstable and Colchester were underpinned by their celebrated native oysters and they are still such significant commodities that each town hosts an annual celebration to honour the opening of the oyster season.

Whitstable Oyster Festival, which includes the annual Blessing of the Waters ceremony, takes place for nine days around 25 July, the feast day of St James, patron saint of oysters. The first catch of oysters is blessed and paraded through town on a wagon drawn by shire horses that deliver the cargo to restaurants, cafes and public houses. A procession walks from St Peter's Church to the seafront to participate in a religious service of thanks for the bounty that comes from the water.

Colchester was the first Roman capital of Britain (the town was called Camulodunum) and the invaders valued native oysters so much that they exported them to Rome. Each year in early September the mayor of Colchester and other civic officials, dressed in their regalia, board a sailing barge for a journey to the Pyefleet Channel to mark the first oyster dredge of the season. In 1189 Richard I sold a charter to Colchester giving them rights over the fishery. Each year since 1540 the Gin and Gingerbread Ceremony has taken place, during which a proclamation is read out to assert the fishing privileges. The mayor raises a loyal toast to the Queen and everyone drinks gin and eats a piece of gingerbread before the first dredge of oysters is made. Before this happens a message is sent to Her Majesty at Balmoral Castle stating that the mayor and councillors will formally proclaim the opening of the Colne oyster fishery for the coming season according to ancient charter. They will drink to her long life and health and send expressions of dutiful loyalty and devotion. Then, with official business out of the way, the party settles down for an oyster lunch.

The Butty

The omnipresent portable foodstuff consisting of a filling between two slices of bread is universally known as the sandwich. It is named after an eighteenth-century English aristocrat called John Montagu, the fourth Earl of Sandwich. Although he did not invent the snack he liked the convenience of eating something quick and easy that did not disturb his sessions at the gambling table.

Classic sarnies, or butties, are bacon (often cited by vegetarians as the one temptation that would make them lapse) and chip butties. And what picnic would be complete without a crisp butty?

How to make the perfect chip butty:

- Only white spongy bread that sticks to the roof of the mouth will do – sliced or tea/barm cakes.
- Thickly butter the bread – margarine does not count.
- Pile the chips on the bread and generously sprinkle with salt and malt vinegar. Ketchup or brown sauce optional.
- Squish the two layers of bread together – this is essential.
- Wash down with a mug of builder's tea.
- Bliss.

Chip butties are not the only starchy delicacy beloved of Britons. Crisps are the most popular snack food throughout the country. Try stuffing them into a cold sandwich. Not only do they add flavour, the crunchy sound effect is irresistible. But potato worship achieves exalted status with bubble and squeak served in a soft white bread roll with a squirt of tangy brown sauce. Bubble (mashed potato) and squeak (usually cabbage) is a traditional method of using up leftovers. The stodgy mixture is fried until crispy on the surface. Its name is believed to refer to the bubbles of water that rise as the potatoes are boiled and the squeak they make as they are fried.

Britain's finest example of bubble in a bun can be found at Maria's Market Café in London's Borough Market. Maria's bubble and squeak is celebrated far and wide and its reputation has even reached Japan, prompting Maria to learn a few phrases of Japanese so she can greet tourists from the Land of the Rising Sun.

The Capital

London is not only the capital city of Britain, it is also the premier financial centre. Londinium was founded as a fortified settlement by Roman invaders in AD 43. That original walled town is now known as the City of London, or the Square Mile. It has always been the heart of commerce and even today the Worshipful Companies that contributed to the wealth of the nation are active, albeit in a different guise. This chapter explains the enduring rituals associated with those ancient trade guilds. A more playful aspect of London is the Pearly lifestyle – those iconic Pearly Kings and Queens resplendent in their unmistakable mother-of-pearl encrusted black suits.

City of London Mysteries

This is not the title of a whodunnit television series set amongst financial traders in the Square Mile; mystery in this case refers to 'professional skill' and is derived from the Latin word *misterium*. London's medieval trade guilds were called mysteries – a combination of trade unions and friendly societies. They began as religious and social fraternities for men who shared the same craft skills. Many guilds later evolved into Worshipful Livery Companies – an echo of their spiritual beginnings. Livery was the apparel worn by various monastic and feudal orders in the Middle Ages. Guild members adopted distinctive gowns to distinguish themselves.

Livery companies wielded great power through control of imports, setting wages and working conditions, training apprentices and upholding trading standards. They were wealthy enough to influence successive kings who often came asking for money to fund overseas wars and lavish lifestyles. Even today governance of the City of London is influenced by livery companies. This anomaly dates from the twelfth century when merchants and citizens of London were granted limited autonomy by the king. Such clout makes Worshipful Companies like no other trade bodies anywhere in the world.

London's trade guilds are unique in that they survive so completely. Currently, there are over a hundred livery companies ranging from the oldest – the Worshipful Company of Bakers and the Worshipful Company of Weavers, to the most recent (founded in 2008) – the Worshipful Company of Security Professionals. Nowadays it is not mandatory for liverymen and women to have a connection to the particular trade associated with their company. Some companies represent crafts that are all but obsolete in Britain but that is no reason for a livery company to cease operation – not when there are fur-trimmed gowns to be worn! Longbows have not been manufactured for centuries in the City, yet the Worshipful Company of Bowyers is still active – but now it encourages the sport of archery rather than makes the equipment.

In several cases, companies continue a regulatory role – Vintners, for instance, are responsible for ensuring European Union wine regulations are implemented. The majority of Worshipful Companies, however, are primarily social and charitable organisations with a particular focus on education, funding schools and bursaries – especially those related to their industry.

The register of Worshipful Companies and Guilds is a snapshot of trades that were once essential to society in medieval Britain and of latter-day industries and service professions that support today's economy. Some have the romance of crafts that are rarely encountered in this country – Armourers, Wax Chandlers – whilst some modern vocations are rather prosaic. What all have in common is a continuation of 1,000 years of guild membership in London and a determination to continue the heritage. See the Appendix for a full list of City of London livery companies.

Livery companies maintain an unbroken link through centuries of London's history as a trading colossus. Their heritage is apparent in street names – Ironmonger Lane, Poultry, Cloth Fair – in City buildings and in several common English phrases. For instance:

Baker's Dozen: a group of thirteen. In the thirteenth century the Bread Assize regulated prices of bread. Bakers would add an extra piece to avoid being accused of selling short measures. The Worshipful Company of Bakers punished those who broke the rules. Penalties included offenders being dragged through the streets with a loaf hanging from their necks.

Hallmark: a distinctive feature. The Goldsmiths' Company assesses the quality of gold and silver and stamps it with an assay mark. Metal craftsmen used to take their work to Goldsmiths' Hall for evaluation.

 At sixes and sevens: in a state of total confusion or disarray. There is an order of precedence of livery companies. A dispute between the Skinners and Merchant Taylors was settled in 1483 with a compromise – the two companies would alternate each year between sixth and seventh in rank. That is still the case today.

Tradition is central to today's companies. They participate in a number of ceremonies – public and private, for example:

Knollys' Red Rose
Each year on 24 June the Master of the Worshipful Company of Watermen and Lightermen cuts a rose from a bush in Seething Lane Gardens. It is placed on an altar cushion and carried by the verger of All Hallows-by-the-Tower in a procession of clergy, parishioners and other officials of the company. The destination is Mansion House – official residence of the Lord Mayor of London. A guard of honour of young watermen dressed in ceremonial Tudor uniforms, each holding an oar, flanks the Lord Mayor as he formally accepts the rose. This ceremony is named after Sir Robert Knollys, a prominent knight and resident of the City of London.

Whist he was away on a military campaign overseas in 1381, his wife Lady Constance supposedly bought a property opposite the family home in Seething Lane. She built a footbridge linking the two buildings but had failed to apply for official authorisation. Anyone else would have been in trouble; however, Sir Robert was such a distinguished citizen that City authorities could hardly punish him. Retrospective planning permission was granted in exchange for a nominal rent of one red rose to be picked from Lady Constance's garden annually on the Feast of St John the Baptist. The bridge disappeared long ago, but the tradition remains.

Cart Marking
Each July up to forty vehicles ranging from hand carts to horse-drawn carriages, from steam wagons to modern articulated lorries, are driven to Guildhall to be formally marked with the year (e.g. 2008) and the coat of arms of the City of London and the Worshipful Company of Carmen. It became law in the fourteenth century that only licensed and marked vehicles were permitted to trade in the City. Nowadays this event is for the sake of tradition only and is significant enough for the Lord Mayor of London to attend.

Vintners' Service at St James Garlickhythe
Vintners attend this annual church service to celebrate the election of the company's new Master in July. The Master and Wardens, dressed in livery gowns and Tudor caps, carry posies and porters sweep the pathway ahead of the procession using birch brooms. This is a tradition to remember their predecessors who would have required flowers to sweeten the foul-smelling air of medieval London and brushes to clear the filth that covered the streets as they left the comfort of Vintners' Hall.

The Doggett Coat and Badge Race
Also in July the Fishmongers, Watermen and Lightermen Companies participate in this popular custom – Britain's oldest annual sporting event, founded in 1715. When actor Thomas Doggett died, his will provided a bequest to pay for a rowing race established in his name. Watermen are licensed to transport passengers and lightermen carry freight on the river Thames.

Any newly licensed waterman or lighterman can compete to row 6.5 kilometres along the Thames from London Bridge to Chelsea Pier. The winner is awarded a scarlet jacket designed to resemble the working dress of an eighteenth-century waterman, and a silver badge. They are presented at Fishmonger's Hall in a fanfare of trumpets and a guard of honour of previous winners resplendent in their prizes.

A Loving Cup

Some companies have a loving cup – an ornate two-handled drinking vessel with a lid – from which members sip wine and toast their neighbour at banquets. The cup is passed round the table in a ritual. As each guest takes their turn they stand up and so does the person on either side of them. One stands with their back to the drinker to repulse an attack, the other faces the drinker, bows and removes the cover from the cup. After a mouthful of wine the cup is passed to the next guest. This procedure is repeated until everyone has drunk from the loving cup. At all times the cup is held with both hands. The rules originated as a security precaution – a way to keep the right 'dagger' hand busy so that everyone may be assured of no treachery, during dinner at least. In 978 King Edward the Martyr was slain with a knife in his back as he drank a cup of mead.

Pearly Kings and Queens in London

Visitors to London may be unaware that the Queen has competition. That's because each borough of the capital has its own royal family in the guise of the pearly kings and queens. They have their own jewels too, although only Elizabeth's are secured in the Tower of London. Pearlies, as they are known, display their valuables on the distinctive costumes that make them icons of London. And rather than diamonds they covet mother-of-pearl. The black outfits they wear are intricately adorned with thousands of mother-of-pearl buttons sewn on by hand to form symbolic patterns. Among them are: horseshoe (luck), anchor (hope), doves (peace), cross (faith), and heart (charity). Even the family dog might sport a specially decorated pearly canine-coat. There are two types of costume: a smother suit covered in buttons and a skeleton suit with fewer buttons and more cloth on show. On their heads the kings wear cheeky caps and the queens model large-brim hats trimmed with flamboyant ostrich feathers.

These splendid Londoners attend all manner of public events decked out in their unmistakeable attire. They are avid charity fundraisers and shake their tins one weekend a month in Covent Garden, delighting tourists with their magical appearance. Some of the livelier members might even sing a verse or two from a traditional song – 'Maybe it's because I'm a Londoner' is always popular. Pearlies require plenty of stamina because the costumes – some beautified with up to 30,000 buttons – can weigh 25 kilograms or more. Places to see them each year are the October harvest festivals at St Paul's Church (Covent Garden), St Mary-le-Bow (Cheapside), St Martin-in-the-Fields (Trafalgar Square), and the Lord Mayor's Show – a procession that winds through the City of London streets in November.

The original pearlies were nineteenth-century cockney costermongers (fruit and vegetable market traders) who showed off their status by decorating their clothes and caps with mother-of-pearl buttons. Historically, pearls were so rare and expensive that only royalty or the wealthiest people could afford them. Long known as the 'Queen of Gems', for thousands of years pearls were revered above all other jewels. The costermongers could not afford real pearls; mother-of-pearl was the next best thing and it showed up well against dark clothing so, crucially, other people could see it and be impressed. Costermongers were a brotherhood who looked after each other when in need. That philanthropic conduct appealed to a young orphaned lad called Henry Croft who had come to know some costermongers because he swept the streets around their market stalls. He copied their style of pearly dress and used his flash appearance to grab the attention of affluent Londoners and raise money from them to help the destitute. Henry's great granddaughter is the pearly queen of Somers Town near Kings Cross. Being a pearly is a family tradition passed down the generations. Modern-day kings and queens, princes and princesses spend a part of their lives in buttons just as their great grandparents did. And it starts early: at pearly christenings the baby has a few buttons sewn on to his/her suit.

Nowadays around one hundred and fifty of Henry's disciples maintain the customs that make pearlies such unique symbols of London.

Mother-of-pearl

Mother-of-pearl, also known as nacre, is the iridescent lining in the shells of certain molluscs including oysters and abalone. Until the 1930s when plastic was invented, the USA was the leading supplier of mother-of-pearl buttons and had served markets around the world including those cockney costermongers of London, the pearlies.

Curiouser and Curiouser

Some traditions are so singular that they defy categorisation. The events in this chapter are utterly unique and range from the public weighing-in of the mayor of High Wycombe before and after he takes office to ensure he works hard, to the Dunmow Flitch Trials in which married couples compete for a side of bacon by trying to persuade a jury that they are in love.

Weighing in of the Mayor in High Wycombe, Buckinghamshire

If an incentive was needed for a public official to lose weight, then High Wycombe has the ultimate motivator: the Weighing in of the Mayor is an annual ceremony to celebrate the election of a new mayor. On the third Saturday in May, newly appointed council members participate in a ritual where they are weighed in full view of the electorate. A weighing seat hangs from a tall brass tripod installed on a platform outside the guildhall. One by one the newly elected mayor dressed in official red robe, black tricorn hat and chain of office, honorary freemen, honorary burgesses, charter trustees and finally the retiring mayor sit on the scales to be weighed. A macebearer in traditional black breeches, frock coat and cocked hat declares the results. It is the outgoing mayor's dimensions that are of greatest interest to spectators. If he or she is heavier than when they entered office the macebearer will state the original weight and then shout 'And some more'. That is the cue for the crowd to jeer. But if the mayor has remained the same or lost a little, the Macebearer calls out 'And no more' to which the audience cheers and claps.

This public humiliation has been a feature of High Wycombe local politics since Victorian times, the inference being that if a mayor piled on the flab they must have been lazy, corrupt and living off the fat of the land at the taxpayers' expense. Mayors who maintained or lost weight had obviously worked hard for the community and deserved applause.

Calling elected officials to account is a speciality of High Wycombe. In 1676 a drunken town burgher made affronts to several gentlemen. In punishment he was stripped of office and the great church bell was tolled to highlight his transgression. Since then it has been customary to ring the church bells for the pronouncement of a new mayor as a reminder that misdemeanours by civic officials will be publicly acknowledged.

So watch out any local councillors who fiddle their expenses or take back-handers – the public is watching and weighing.

Wycombe – Not Always High

The name Wycombe derives from the river Wye and 'combe', the old English word for a wooded valley. A settlement was first documented in 970 as Wicumun. As late as 1911 the town was known as Chepping or Chipping Wycombe.

Old Man's Day in Braughing, Hertfordshire

Old Man's Day would never have happened were it not for the slimy autumn leaves that covered Fleece Lane one autumn day in the mid-sixteenth century. As a coffin was being carried to St Mary the Virgin church, a pallbearer slipped and the cask fell on the ground. Inside it, a young man who had died without warning was jolted back to life. Shocked mourners stared in disbelief as a confused but otherwise healthy Matthew Wall emerged from the box.

Matthew managed to delay his real funeral well into old age. In 1595 his will contained a bequest to the village. He left money to pay for a poor man to sweep Fleece Lane clear of those pesky leaves each year on 2 October, the anniversary of his resurrection. Matthew also stipulated that the church bells be rung – first a funeral toll, and then a wedding peal in celebration of his marriage soon after that miraculous return from the dead. On his grave he asked for brambles to be planted to prevent sheep grazing there.

Old Man's Day is now marked every year by the community but instead of hiring a man with no money, a group of local adults and school children armed with brooms meet to sweep the lane. The bells ring out just as Matthew instructed and a short service takes place by his graveside where no sheep dare tread.

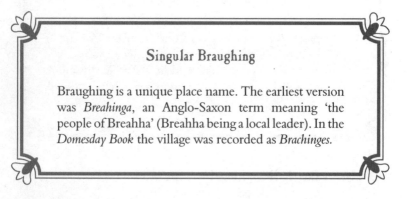

Singular Braughing

Braughing is a unique place name. The earliest version was *Breahinga*, an Anglo-Saxon term meaning 'the people of Breahha' (Breahha being a local leader). In the *Domesday Book* the village was recorded as *Brachinges*.

The Wroth Silver Ceremony in Ryton-on-Dunsmore, Warwickshire

It is an early start for parish representatives of the Knightlow Hundreds on 11 November when a pre-dawn ceremony takes place at Knightlow Cross. The congregants are there to pay annual dues known as 'wroth silver' to local landowner, the Duke of Buccleuch and Queensberry. The Duke's agent reads out the charter of assembly, which states:

> *Wroth silver due to his Grace the Duke of Buccleuch and payable at Knightlow Cross on Martinmas Eve, 11 November… before sun-rising. Non-payment thereof forfeiture of 100 pence for every penny, or a white bull with red ears and red nose.*

Bulls with Red Noses

The white bull with a red nose and red ears mentioned in the charter of assembly is likely to be a white park, the most ancient native cattle breed in Britain. They have been a status symbol for centuries and were considered so precious by the government that a number of white parks were transported to King Ranch in Texas at the start of World War Two in order to preserve part of the national heritage.

A list of twenty-five parishes in the Knightlow Hundreds (a hundred is the ancient term for an administrative region) is read out. One at a time, the delegates step forward and say 'wroth silver' as they drop a coin or two into the hollow on a flat stone that was once the base of a medieval way cross. Not all parishes pay the same amount. Birdingbury and Barnacle get away with a penny; Bubbenhall and Toft pay tuppence ha'penny, whereas Harbury has to fork out two shillings threepence ha'penny. In today's money the total is around 46 pence.

After the dues have been paid the assembly goes to a nearby pub for a slap-up breakfast and toasts the duke with a warming tot of rum with hot milk. They take away with them a churchwarden's tobacco pipe as a memento. In the years before smoking was banned in public places, the group used to light up their clay pipes.

It is not clear how the wroth silver custom came into being, but the organisers believe it is England's oldest continuous custom (with a short break in the reign of Queen Victoria). A written record in 1170 implied that the tradition was already ongoing. The word 'wroth' is also a mystery. In the thirteenth century the term 'warth-penny' was used in the region. Records from 1628 refer to 'the wroth monies'. The most likely explanation is that wroth silver was rent paid to the landowner for common grazing rights. The duke and representatives of the Knightlow Hundreds continue it for the sake of tradition.

Wilkes Walk in Leighton Buzzard, Bedfordshire

In many British towns and cities, almshouses serve as a reminder of the philanthropists who gave a home to people in need. At the time they were built, such dwellings were considered to be modest, but today some of them are noteworthy enough to be on the English Heritage Listed Buildings Register. The first recorded almshouses were built in York and paid for by King Athelstan in the tenth century. Today there are 2,600 groups of almshouses that provide affordable housing for elderly people.

Edward Wilkes was a generous benefactor who funded almshouses in 1630 to provide homes for ten poor widows in Leighton Buzzard. His son Matthew wanted to ensure that his father's generosity was commemorated by future generations and so he included a specific clause in his own will of 1693. It stipulated that church officials were to gather outside the almshouses where one of them would hold a child upside down as an extract of Edward's last will and testament was read out – the theory being that everyone would understand the significance of the bequest better if they knew the blood was running into the head of a topsy-turvy little boy.

More than 300 years on and this annual rite still takes place. On Rogation Monday (following the fifth Sunday after Easter) clergy and choir from All Saints Church partake in the Wilkes

Walk Procession and the Ceremony of Upending. Prayers are said and hymns are sung outside the almshouses – then comes the upending. An altar cushion is laid on the pavement and one of the shorter choir members volunteers to perform a handstand with his or her head resting on the cushion while the priest clutches their ankles to prevent them falling over. Lines from Edward's will are recited after which the choir boy/girl is turned the right way up.

Money from the Wilkes bequest is distributed to residents of the almshouses, to the choir for their angelic singing and most importantly to the child who performed the acrobatics. Afterwards everyone is invited for refreshments. This treat used to be ale and spiced buns consumed at the market cross but that ceased in 1896 when the word got out and hundreds of people turned up and drank the free beer dry.

A Bird of Pray?

Leighton Buzzard's unusual name is thought to have originated in the twelfth century from the Old English word for a clearing in the woods (leighton) and a corruption of the surname of Thomas de Busar, a local clergyman.

Dunmow Flitch Trials in Great Dunmow, Essex

People driving through the Essex countryside might wonder at the town sign welcoming visitors to 'Great Dunmow – Home of the Flitch Trials'. If they returned in July of a leap year they could watch as five couples publicly declared that in 'twelvemonth and a day' they have 'not wisht themselves unmarried again'.

There is a prize for proving such ardour, but not champagne, roses or chocolates – the reward is a side of bacon, or flitch. But in order to win the tasty trophy the couple must prove their allegiance. That means standing trial in a mock courtroom with a judge, prosecution and defence counsel, a jury of six young bachelors and six young maidens, a clerk of the court, an usher to maintain order and a public gallery.

The Dunmow Flitch Trials is an ancient ceremony alleged to date to the twelfth century when the lord of the manor and his wife disguised themselves and asked the local prior to bless their union of a year and a day. The monk was so impressed by the couple's dedication to each other he rewarded them with a side of bacon. Even before the era of mass media, the Dunmow Flitch Trials was widely known. Chaucer refers to it in *The Canterbury Tales* when the irrepressible Wife of Bath ironically asserts that none of her five husbands would have dreamt of claiming the flitch. A couple of decades earlier (1360s) William Langland mentioned the trials in his poem 'The Vision of Piers Plowman'.

Any married couple can apply to be judged on the strength of their union. Applications are vetted and five couples with a compelling story are chosen to attend trial. People who have faced adversity that has tested their commitment to marriage are ideal candidates. One previous winning couple described an air raid during their 1939 wedding ceremony that prompted the vicar to run from the church in terror. They managed to coax him back but he rushed through the formalities in just over three minutes and fled. Four days after the wedding the groom was called up to military service overseas and his bride did not see him again for six years. Despite that shaky start the marriage prevailed for over fifty years.

Before the tests begin the town crier escorts a procession of Flitch Trial officials to the marquee where the court sits. Ahead of the parade the flitch hangs on a frame adorned with green foliage borne ceremoniously on the shoulders of a group of men dressed in medieval peasant smocks and hats trimmed with flowers. Following the crowd are several similarly attired serfs who carry the ancient wooden Flitch Chair for the winning couple (known as claimants) to sit in.

There are separate trials for each of the five couples with sessions starting in the morning and running through the afternoon and into the evening. They may be mock trials but the legal proceedings are authentic. Members of counsel are often real barristers and wear the grey horsehair wigs and black gowns of their profession, and the judge is in the full horsehair wig and robes that reflect his office. Knowledge of how a trial works is preferable for all the officials but a sense of humour is essential. The jury, sworn in just as it would be in a real trial, is comprised of eighteen-year-old school pupils (maidens in white dresses and hats and carrying posies, bachelors in dark suits and ties).

Each couple sits together on the stand to be questioned by prosecution and defence barristers and try to convey their attachment to each other. Counsel for the flitch donors (two local butchers) aim to prevent the pork being given away by challenging statements of devotion and raise reasonable doubt in the jury. When all the evidence has been heard the jury retires to consider the facts and try to reach a unanimous verdict. Most couples do end up winning a flitch but in some cases the jury will not be convinced. The unsuccessful ones do not leave empty handed, though – they take away a joint of gammon. But as a public acknowledgment of their also-ran status they are forced to walk through the streets behind the empty Flitch Chair. Oh, the shame.

None of that humiliation for the flitch winners. After each trial the successful couple is carried in the Flitch Chair on the shoulders of 'eight humble folk' to Market Place for the oath-taking ceremony. Mr and Mrs kneel down on stones and the vicar asks them to repeat the Flitch Oath:

You Do Swear By Custom Of Confession
That You Ne'er Made Nuptual Transgression
Nor Since You Were Married Man And Wife
By Household Brawls Or Contentious Strife
Or Otherwise In Bed Or At Board
Offended Each Other In Deed Or In Word
Or In A Twelve Months Time And A Day
Repented Not In Thought In Any Way
Or Since The Church Clerk Said Amen
Wish't Yourselves Unmarried Again
But Continue True And Desire
As When You Joined Hands In Holy Quire.

A Big Enough Bag

Winners do not need to provide a pig-shaped bag to carry the flitch home in – the butchers who donate the bacon cut it into small joints.

Several extant documents, the earliest in 1445, record the proceedings of the trials. One of them outlines the instance in 1832 when a retired cheese-monger called Josiah Vine from Reading applied to be tried. The judge sniffily refused the application and reportedly said that he considered the trials to be 'an idle custom bringing people of indifferent character into the neighbourhood'. On another occasion in the nineteenth century a winning couple was overheard arguing after they had won the flitch. It was promptly confiscated, cut up and shared amongst the other claimants. So the lesson is: keep smiling if you want to bring home the bacon.

Appendix: The City of London Livery Companies

The City of London livery companies represent the ancient and modern crafts and industries practised over the centuries in the City. Most company titles include the word 'Worshipful', although this is not a mandatory moniker – it is up to each company how it styles itself.

In the past there were two ways a guild was recognised as a livery company – either by permission of the monarch, or by the City of London authorities. The dates quoted in each entry refer to the earliest guild records, or to the year the company was granted livery status, or when it received its first royal charter. In several cases guilds existed for centuries before officially becoming livery companies. The Great Fire of London in 1666 destroyed countless records so it is not possible to be accurate about every founding date.

All the companies exist now to provide fellowship, to support the traditions of the City, to raise money for charity, and in many cases to promote education and research. Some of them are actively connected with aspects of their particular trade and perform a regulatory role.

In alphabetical order:

The Brewers' Company
Beer is of great importance in Britain for many reasons. Historically, where pollution made water unsafe, to drink beer was a safe substitute. This was especially so in London. The company's original name was 'The Master and Keepers or Wardens and Commonality of the Mystery or Art of Brewers in the City of London.' Today, membership is confined to directors of brewing companies and the company actively supports the brewing industry in south-east England. Its first royal charter was granted in 1437.

The Carpenters' Company
The company received its first royal charter in 1477. Its influence over the building trade started to wane after the Great Fire of London in 1666 when brick and stone replaced timber as the City was rebuilt. The Carpenters' Company established the Trades Training School in 1893, now called the Building Crafts College, which educates people in the craft of woodwork.

The Chartered Surveyors' Company
The majority of liverymen and women in this company are chartered surveyors, and if not they are leading members of the property profession. Founded in 1977.

The City of London Solicitors' Company
The Solicitors' Company, founded in 1908, has a strict membership policy – members are required to practise or to have practised as a solicitor within one mile of the Bank of England or at Canary Wharf.

The Clothworkers' Company
Much of the wealth of medieval England was based on wool and textile exports, so the skills of clothworkers were very much in demand. The company received a royal charter in 1528 but existed before then with the name of 'the Guild or Fraternity of the Assumption of the Blessed Virgin Mary of Clothworkers in the City of London'.

The Company of Watermen and Lightermen
The company was established by an Act of Parliament in 1555 to control the watermen on the River Thames. Until 1750, when Westminster Bridge was constructed, London Bridge was the only Thames crossing in London. People were dependent on watermen rowing them between the north and south banks. Today the company is responsible for examining and licensing those working on the tidal river Thames. Watermen ferry humans and lightermen move cargo (a lighter is a barge).

The Drapers' Company
The full title is 'The Master and Wardens and Brethren and Sisters of the Guild or Fraternity of the Blessed Mary the Virgin of the Mystery of Drapers of the City of London'. An informal association of drapers existed as early as 1180 but the

first royal charter was granted in 1364. With the growth of the English woollen cloth trade in the fifteenth century the Drapers' Company prospered because of the strict control it retained over the sale of cloth.

The Guild of Air Pilots and Air Navigators

Membership is restricted to qualified pilots and navigators. The company promotes good airmanship. Members have flown all types of aircraft, ranging from supersonic fighter jets to hot air balloons. It was founded in 1956.

The Haberdashers' Company

Haberdashers sold ribbons, beads, purses, gloves, pins, caps and toys. The first written mention of a guild of haberdashers is from 1371. The company was given a royal charter in 1448. Today the company is a leading educational trust with nine schools around the country (private and state) and is a generous charitable organisation.

The Honourable Company of Master Mariners

Membership is open to master mariners from the merchant navy and Royal Navy. The company was formed in 1926 to promote high standards of professional conduct, to maintain friendship between the two branches of the navy, to provide advice when necessary on issues affecting the merchant navy, and to support education and charity.

The Ironmongers' Company

The earliest records in 1300 referred to the guild as the ferroners (from the Latin word for iron *ferrum*) and soon after they were described as the 'Honourable Crafte and Fellasship of Fraunchised Men of Iromongers'. The company's royal charter was awarded in 1463.

APPENDIX

The Leathersellers' Company
Documentary evidence of a leathersellers' guild appears in 1372 when the members lobbied to protect their craft against the issue of fake goods. Sheep leather was being sold as the more durable roe leather and it gave everyone in that business a bad name.

The mainstay of the leathersellers' trade was points – leather laces for fastening armour and clothing. A royal charter was issued to the company in 1444.

The Masons' Company
Not to be confused with the Freemasons fraternal organisation, although members of the Masons' Company may also be Freemasons. A royal charter was not issued until 1677, despite the earliest record of a stonemasons' guild dating back to 1356. Over the years, members would have been responsible for the construction of the City's significant buildings, including St Paul's cathedral. Two former masters of the company worked as stonemasons on St Paul's under the direction of Sir Christopher Wren.

The Mercers' Company
Mercers were originally involved in mercery – the export of woollen materials and the import of silk, linen, and cloth of gold, a textile that was spun with a gold thread. The company was formed by royal charter in 1394. Dick Whittington was a successful mercer who supplied King Richard II with luxury fabrics. When the king was deposed in 1399 he owed Whittington £1,000 – in today's money that is £408,000. The mercers are number one in the livery company rank.

The Merchant Taylors' Company
The 'Gild of Merchant Taylors of the Fraternity of St John Baptist in the City of London' was formed by tailors and linen armourers

– craftsmen who made the padded tunics (gambesons) worn under suits of armour. It was founded in 1327.

The Salters' Company
When the guild was formed in 1394, salt was the only means of preserving meat. Salters supplied a vital commodity. They also dealt in flax, hemp, cochineal and potash. Today, the company is active in charity work – this includes funding the Salters' Institute to promote science education.

The Skinners' Company
Skinners traded in fur. Richer members of society wore garments that were trimmed or lined with fur. Ermine and sable (expensive imported furs) were reserved for the aristocracy. Common folk had to make do with home-grown lambskin, rabbit fur and cat fur. The company was founded in 1327.

The Vintners' Company
The Vintners' Company was first granted a charter in 1364 when it was responsible for the import, regulation and sale of wine. Wine was important to the medieval economy, forming a significant percentage of England's import trade. In recent years the vintners' have been responsible for ensuring that European Union wine legislation regulations are implemented through its Wine Standards Board.

The Worshipful Company of Actuaries
Membership is restricted to actuaries (business analysts). The company, founded in 1979, is actively involved in financial services. Nowadays that is the City's prime industry.

The Worshipful Company of Arbitrators
Founded in 1981, the company is comprised of professionals involved in dispute resolution, and it actively supports the discipline.

APPENDIX

The Worshipful Company of Armourers and Brasiers
In 1322, the Guild of St George of the Armourers was formed. The first royal charter was granted in 1453. Brasiers (brass and copper workers) were associated with the company as early as the sixteenth century and were given equal status in a royal charter issued in 1708.

During the centuries when soldiers wore armour, members of the guild often travelled with the army into battle, to make new armour or repair damaged kit.

Today, the company no longer makes armour but it retains close links with the armed forces by awarding prizes to promising military personnel. It is also a leading charity, supporting education in metallurgy and materials science.

The Worshipful Company of Bakers
Many current members are master bakers. In the medieval period the guild had the legal power to punish any baker who sold short weights or adulterated bread (sawdust and sand were common taints). For a first offence the offender would be dragged through the streets with the sub-standard loaf hanging from his neck. For a second offence he spent an hour in the pillory, and if the baker had still not learned and he broke the law again, his oven was destroyed. Records date back to 1155.

The Worshipful Company of Barbers
For centuries, barbers not only groomed hair and shaved their customers; they also performed surgical tasks, including dentistry. At the time when blood-letting with leeches was a common medical procedure, barbers were permitted to administer it. The red-and-white-striped pole outside a barber's shop may be connected with this practice. It has been suggested that customers would grip the pole to increase blood flow.

Today's company has no connection with hairdressing but has links with surgery and medicine. One of its main charitable objectives is to support the Phyllis Tuckwell Hospice in Farnham, providing palliative care to adults with life-limiting illnesses. Company records date back to 1308.

The Worshipful Company of Basketmakers

From the fifteenth century, basket making in London was concentrated around the parish of St Margaret Pattens in Great Tower Street. Baskets were not just used to carry the shopping home in – they took numerous other forms, including boats (coracles), houses (wattle), or buckets. Today, the company supports the craft of basket making through education. It was founded in 1569.

The Worshipful Company of Blacksmiths

A blacksmith forges molten metal and uses tools to shape it into products such as railings, furniture, wrought-iron gates and furniture. Those skills are still in demand today. The company champions this craft by providing a directory of working smiths, and by encouraging young people to take up apprenticeships. Early members of the guild included tooth drawers (dentists). Written references to the company date back to 1325.

The Worshipful Company of Bowyers

Gone are the times when all able-bodied Englishmen between the ages of sixteen and sixty were bidden by royal decree to practise their archery skills on Sundays. It was that talent with a bow and arrow that made England's medieval archers such a fearsome military force. Members of The Worshipful Company of Bowyers crafted the longbows that beat French soldiers at the battles of Agincourt, Crecy and Poitiers. Today, the company encourages people to take part in the sport of archery. The company was founded in 1363.

The Worshipful Company of Broderers

The Brotherhood of The Holy Ghost of the City of London, better known as the Worshipful Company of Broderers, was formed in the thirteenth century and was granted its first royal charter in 1561. The golden age of embroidery was 1250–1350, when 'English work' or *opus anglicanum* was exported all over Europe. *Opus anglicanum* was celebrated for fine goldwork and the skilful use of complicated stitching. Today, few members are actual embroiderers but the company supports the craft in several ways, including backing an apprentice scheme at the Royal School of Needlework.

The Worshipful Company of Builders' Merchants

Founded in 1961 to enhance the status, dignity and prestige of the builders' merchant. Historically, membership was confined to those in the building merchant profession but today it includes people who are closely associated with the industry.

The Worshipful Company of Butchers

Records indicate that an informal organisation of butchers existed in 975. Each year in December the company presents a boar's head to the Lord Mayor. This tradition started in 1469 as payment for land that the company did business on. The company's motto is *Omnia Subjecisti Sub Pedibus, Oves et Boves*: Thou hast put all things under his feet, all Sheep and Oxen. A royal charter was first granted in 1605.

The Worshipful Company of Carmen

In 1517 the carmen formed a guild called 'the Fraternyte of Seynt Katryne the Virgyn and Marter of Carters'. The members were men who carried goods and people by surface transportation – that usually meant by horse and cart or carriage. In today's company the members still have links with transport. Activities today include the presentation of lectures about modern issues related to transport at the Royal Society for the Encouragement of Arts, Manufactures and Commerce.

The Worshipful Company of Chartered Accountants in England and Wales

The company's principal objective is to champion the profession of accountancy and to promote honourable practice. It is one of the companies that were formed in the 1970s (this one in 1977) at a time when it had become apparent that many livery companies had no direct connections with the industry of the modern City – financial services.

The Worshipful Company of Chartered Architects

The company was granted livery status in 1988 and exists to advance the influence of the profession of architecture. Its charitable work is mainly focused on architectural education and scholarship.

The Worshipful Company of Chartered Secretaries and Administrators

Livery status was granted in 1977. Aims of the company include enhancing the profession (chartered secretaries are qualified in corporate law, finance and governance), particularly in the City of London.

The Worshipful Company of Clockmakers of London

The Company of Clockmakers is the world's oldest existing horological institution. Its museum in London's Guildhall contains the oldest extant collection of clocks, watches and sundials. The majority of its members are still involved in horology. It was founded by royal charter in 1631.

APPENDIX

The Worshipful Company of Coachmakers and Coach Harness Makers of London
Formerly responsible for quality control in the craft of coach making, today the company supports the heritage of coach and coach harness making by promoting excellence in modern-day carriages; that is, the auto, rail and aerospace industries. The company received its charter in 1677 but it had existed for years previous to that date.

The Worshipful Company of Constructors
The Company of Constructors' gained livery status in 1990. It supports education and training in the profession. Members are professionals from or associated with the construction industry.

The Worshipful Company of Cooks
The Company of Cooks, founded in 1482, was an amalgamation of three guilds – the Cooks, Pastlers (pasty makers) and Piebakers. The company wardens had the power to examine the business premises of cooks and to punish them for selling bad food. A common punishment was to send the miscreant to the pillory where the offending victuals were burnt under him. Many company members today still have connections with the catering industry.

The Worshipful Company of Coopers
A cooper is a person who makes or repairs wooden caskets and barrels. Demand for the coopers' craft has waned as metal beer casks have all but replaced wooden ones in the brewing industry. A royal charter was granted to the company in 1501, although the coopers had an existing craft guild that dated back to at least 1298.

The Worshipful Company of Cordwainers
The word 'cordwainer', meaning shoemaker, derives from the Spanish *cordobán,* referring to the ancient Spanish leatherworking centre of Cordoba. A royal charter was issued in 1439 but the guild existed as early as 1272. The company supports education and training, most notably at Cordwainers College in Hackney (established by the company in 1887) where students study footwear design and manufacture, and the design and production of leather goods and saddlery.

The Worshipful Company of Curriers
Curriers hand prepare and dress tanned leather – the skill is still required for producing equestrian equipment. The company was founded in 1580 but the guild existed in 1282. The majority of London curriers worked around Farringdon Road and Fleet Street because the Smithfield meat market and several abattoirs located nearby provided them with a supply of animal hides. In Medieval England, curriers were busy supplying the army – relentless war with Scotland and later with France meant that soldiers needed leather to line armour and for items of clothing.

The Worshipful Company of Cutlers
The word 'cutler' is derived from the old French *coutelier* and means a maker or seller of implements with a cutting edge. Although cutlers traded in all manner of cutting instruments such as knives and razors, it was their skill at producing fighting weapons that brought them prosperity. A royal charter was issued in 1416, although records date the guild back to the thirteenth century.

The Worshipful Company of Distillers
When the company was granted a royal charter in 1638 it was given the power to regulate the spirits distilling trade within 21

miles of London. That perquisite no longer applies and today the company is a social and charitable organisation with many members who work in the spirits industry, wine trade or have a connection to the drinks business.

The Worshipful Company of Dyers

The skills of craft dyers were much in demand during the centuries when textile exports were such valuable commodities. A guild was formalised in 1310 and the livery company royal charter issued in 1471. The company's present day activities are focused on education and development of the craft of dyeing, particularly through the Department of Colour Chemistry at Leeds University and the Society of Dyers and Colourists in Bradford.

The Worshipful Company of Engineers

Members of this livery company (formed in 2004) are all chartered engineers or fellows of the Royal Academy of Engineering. The company works to promote the science and practice of engineering.

The Worshipful Company of Environmental Cleaners

The company was founded in 1986 and the motto is *Tergere est Servare*, meaning 'to clean is to preserve'. Its patron saint is St Martha, sister of Lazarus and Mary. When Jesus visited her house she complained to him that Mary had not helped clean the house sufficiently.

The Worshipful Company of Fan Makers

The Company of Fan Makers was formed to protect the craft of English fan making from the threat of cheap foreign imports. It was issued a royal charter in 1709. Fans were the height of fashion in England between 1750 and 1800 and in those years the company was busy protecting the interests of its members from inferior workmanship of imported fans. In modern times, the company has links with the mechanical fan trade for ventilation and engine cooling.

The Worshipful Company of Farmers
A grant of livery was approved in 1952. Two of the company's main objectives are to stimulate the development of agricultural education and to promote an appreciation of the importance of farming to the economic health of the nation.

The Worshipful Company of Farriers
The farriers' guild was established in 1356 to oversee farriery in London. By 1674 it had been granted a royal charter. Today the company is as relevant as ever because, by law, horses must be shod by skilled and registered persons. The Company of Farriers has a legal duty to ensure standards of competence and conduct in those who shoe horses.

The Worshipful Company of Feltmakers of London
Feltmaking was mentioned as a trade in 1180, but it was 1604 before a royal charter granting livery status was issued to this company. Today the company supplies the official black-feathered tricorn hat worn by each new Lord Mayor of London. The Scriveners and Glovers Companies provide the quill and gloves.

The Worshipful Company of Firefighters
Founded in 1988, the main objective of the company is to promote fire prevention and safety, and the development and advancement of the science and practice of fire fighting.

The Worshipful Company of Fishmongers
Amongst the most ancient of all the guilds, the fishmongers were organised long before the first royal charter was granted

in 1272. Until the Reformation (from around 1527) the Catholic church decreed that meat consumption was forbidden on certain days, and fish was the alternative. That made the fishmongers very powerful and wealthy.

Ever since 1604 officials of the company (known as fishmeters) have had the authority to examine all fish in Billingsgate Market to ensure quality. If they discover bad fish on sale, the company institutes legal proceedings under the Food and Drugs Act of 1955.

The Worshipful Company of Fletchers

Fletchers make arrows, and though they are no longer produced in the City of London the traditions of the company continue. The company awards certificates of excellence in the craft. Fletchers present a box of finished arrows that are checked for length, weight, balance and spine – a procedure not dissimilar to the medieval apprentice presenting his best work at the end of his apprenticeship. The first record of a guild of fletchers is in 1371. Members made arrows for the 100 Years War with France and later the Wars of the Roses.

The Worshipful Company of Founders

Founders worked with brass and brass alloys or tinplate to cast pots, pans and candlesticks. An early written record about a guild of founders dates back to 1365. The company had a lucrative secondary trade in the production of brass weights used for weighing goods. To inspire consumer confidence, the founders were given the task of assizing weights brought in by retailers and ensuring they were accurate and had not been tampered with to enable short measures.

The Worshipful Company of Framework Knitters

Framework knitters are specialists in the craft of knitting and hosiery. The company was founded in 1657. Today its main functions are to support its charities in educational bursaries, and to maintain a group of almshouses at Oadby in Leicestershire for retired knitting workers (the knitting industry eventually grew to be centred around Leicester and Nottingham).

The Worshipful Company of Fruiterers

This company received a royal charter in 1605 but it had existed for centuries before then. One of its responsibilities was to inspect all fruit entering the City and assess the duty. Each autumn the company presents a gift of fruit to the Lord Mayor of London to commemorate the abolition of tolls payable on fruit entering London. The fruiterers' charity ensures that fruit is distributed each month to hostels for the homeless.

The Worshipful Company of Fuellers

Granted livery status under its present name in 1984, the company can trace its origins back to the woodmongers' guild in the fourteenth century. Today membership is restricted to those engaged in the energy industry – fossil fuels, nuclear and renewable.

The Worshipful Company of Furniture Makers

Founded in 1963 the company exists to support furniture design, manufacture, marketing and retailing. It facilitates training and awards Guild Marks for Excellence to inspire confidence in British craftsmen and women.

The Worshipful Company of Gardeners

The gardeners existed for centuries as a fellowship before being recognised as a livery company in 1605. Today, its aims are to promote good gardening, and to beautify the City of London by encouraging the display of flowers and foliage wherever possible.

The Worshipful Company of Girdlers

When this guild was founded in 1327 (and later as a livery company in 1449) girdles were not the undergarments worn today to flatten down the belly; they were a fashion accessory more like a long belt that hung from the waist, over the hips and down the front of the clothing. They were often made from linen, leather or metal and heavily decorated with jewels or buckles.

The Worshipful Company of Glass-Sellers and Looking-Glass Makers of London

Other glass-related companies such as the Worshipful Company of Glaziers and Painters of Glass already existed when the Glass-Sellers was founded in 1664. What this new guild did was to regulate the trade in drinking vessels and tableware, looking glasses and glass vials. Its role today is one of fellowship and charity.

The Worshipful Company of Glaziers and
Painters of Glass

There is evidence that the glaziers' guild existed as early as 1328. Back then glass was a luxury item, important for letting in light to a building whilst keeping the weather out. Today, the company is active in all aspects of stained glass, including assisting the relocation of historic glass from deconsecrated churches to other churches or suitable public buildings.

The Worshipful Company of Glovers of London

The Company of Glovers was formed in 1349. One of the rules for guild members was that no gloves were to be sold by candlelight – it was important that the customer should be able to see the excellent quality. Many of today's members have connections with the British glove industry and the company encourages glove wearing. The glovers own a collection of rare gloves, some dating back to the sixteenth century, embroidered with silks, seed pearls, ribbons and metallic lace. They are in the care of the Fashion Museum in Bath and a selection is always on public view.

The Worshipful Company of Gold and Silver Wyre Drawers

Wyre drawers practise the art of embroidering with gold and silver thread to decorate badges, banners, vestments, service uniforms and officials' gowns. A guild was established in 1423 but livery status was not awarded until 1780. The company funds the education of an apprentice each year at the Royal School of Needlework and presents a prize for the best work in gold and silver wire.

The Worshipful Company of Goldsmiths

Since 1300 the Company of Goldsmiths has been responsible for assaying (testing for purity) gold and silver wares. Today, the company runs the London Assay Office, where several million articles of gold, silver and platinum are hallmarked each year.

The Worshipful Company of Grocers

This was originally known as The Guild of Pepperers, and records of it date from 1180. The occasional use of pepper as a currency gave rise to the phrase 'peppercorn rent'. Members traded goods 'in gross' and in 1376 changed the name of the guild to 'The Company of Grossers of London'.

The Worshipful Company of Gunmakers

The company received a royal charter in 1637. Today it has the responsibility for ensuring that guns sold in Britain are safe to fire. Many of its members are connected with the gun-making trade.

The Worshipful Company of Hackney Carriage Drivers

This was founded as a livery company in 2004, and its members must be taxi drivers. These drivers are licensed and tend to drive the vehicles commonly known as black cabs. In order to drive a hackney cab and gain a licence, drivers must pass 'the Knowledge', a rigorous exam where they are tested on the location of streets and landmarks within a 10-kilometre radius of Charing Cross. It can take three years of training to achieve this feat.

The Worshipful Company of Horners

Horners worked with animal horn – the plastic of its day – to make buckles, combs and beakers. Early references to the guild were written in 1284. The bottlemakers joined in 1476 and the company was issued with a royal charter in 1638. The modern horners' company supports those ancient crafts and also promotes the interests and developments of the plastics industry.

The Worshipful Company of Information Technologists

Representing one of the key industries of the twenty-first century, this livery company was founded in 1992. Members are all leading IT practitioners. The aims of the company are fellowship and to support charities by providing IT expertise.

The Worshipful Company of Innholders

Inns played a central role during the thirteenth century when they provided refreshment and shelter to pilgrims and traders (and their horses). Then, the people who ran the inns were known as hostellers or hospitalers. They became known as the guild of innholders in 1473 and received a royal charter in 1514.

The Worshipful Company of Insurers

Insurance is big business in the City of London so a livery company was formed in 1979 to reflect the importance of that industry. Membership is limited to people who are engaged in the insurance profession.

The Worshipful Company of International Bankers
Arguably the most cosmopolitan of all the livery companies, members of this guild comprise more than forty nationalities. It was founded in 2004 and is associated with banking – one of the major industries in the City.

The Worshipful Company of Joiners and Ceilers of the City of London
The joiners and ceilers represented the craft of woodwork. Its members were separate from the carpenters because they had different skills. Joiners and ceilers used glue or similar to join pieces of wood together whereas carpenters used nails. The company was issued with a royal charter in 1571.

The Worshipful Company of Launderers
The company's motto is 'Cleanliness is next to Godliness'. A domestic cat appears on the coat of arms, cats being considered the cleanest of creatures. It was founded in 1978.

The Worshipful Company of Lightmongers
One of the modern livery companies – it was founded in 1979. Members come from all sections of the lighting and electrical industries.

The Worshipful Company of Loriners
A loriner makes and sells bits, bridles, spurs and stirrups for horses. The word derives from the Latin *lorum* meaning a strap, thong, bridle or reins. In 1711 a royal charter formalised the loriners as a livery company, although the guild had existed since at least 1261.

APPENDIX

The Worshipful Company of Makers of Playing Cards
The company was founded by royal charter in 1628 as the 'Mistery of Makers of Playing Cards of the City of London'. Its purpose was to regulate the trade of playing card manufacture and to ensure that each pack was sealed and duty paid to the king. In exchange for this agreement, customs officers seized cheaper foreign imports and kept them off the market.

The Worshipful Company of Management Consultants
A modern livery company, founded in 2004, that aims to support the profession of consultancy, to contribute to the traditions of the City and to raise money for charity.

The Worshipful Company of Marketors
The company aims to maintain high standards in the business of marketing – one way it does this is with its think tank, a forum that reports on issues that matter to the profession. The company was formed in 1978.

The Worshipful Company of Musicians
Members of the company are performers, composers, instrument makers and music teachers. Its aims are to support young musicians at the start of their careers by giving prizes and scholarships, provide opportunities for performance, and award medals that recognise excellence and achievement. The company was founded in 1604.

The Worshipful Company of Needlemakers
The needlemakers are one of only two existing companies that received their charter (1656) from Oliver Cromwell when he was Lord Protector – the other one is the Worshipful Company of Framework Knitters. The skill of London's medieval embroiderers was celebrated, but to achieve such intricate

work they required fine needles, and that is why the craft of the needlemakers was important.

The Worshipful Company of Painter-Stainers

Painters decorated, gilded and coloured solid objects made of wood, metal and stone, and stainers applied colour to woven fabrics. The earliest reference to a guild of stainers is in 1268, and to the painters in 1283. They united in 1502 to form the Worshipful Company of Painter-Stainers.

The Worshipful Company of Parish Clerks

Members do not wear livery because parish clerks were originally of religious orders and already wore clerical garb. The membership is restricted to men and women of the Church of England who serve in one of the 150 parishes associated with the company. Royal charters were granted by a number of monarchs beginning in 1442 (Henry VI) and the final one in 1639 (Charles I), which described the company as: 'The Master, Wardens, Assistants and Brethren of the Parish Clerks of the City and Suburbs of London and the Liberties thereof, the City of Westminster, the Borough of Southwark and the fifteen out-parishes adjacent.'

The Worshipful Company of Pattenmakers

Pattens were wooden or metal contraptions strapped beneath the wearer's shoes to raise them out of the filth of the streets. Trade declined with the paving of the roads and the last working pattenmaker is thought to have died in the nineteenth century. The company received a royal charter in 1670.

The Worshipful Company of Paviors

Paviors were responsible for the repair and cleaning of London's streets from 1280 and the company was formally established in 1479. In the absence of flushing lavatories the company had a lucrative sideline called 'going ferming'– the emptying and cleaning of privies. Today a large percentage of company members are associated with highways and construction.

The Worshipful Company of Pewterers

Pewter is a metal alloy usually composed of tin and copper. It was a cheap substitute for silver and china, and pewterers produced tableware, drinking vessels and ornaments. The earliest documented reference to the pewterers' guild is dated 1348. The company renewed its connection with the craft in 1970 and since then it has worked to train pewtersmiths, and to improve the quality of pewter wares.

The Worshipful Company of Plaisterers

London's plasterers would have been very much in demand in 1189 following an order from the Lord Mayor of London that all houses should be plastered and lime-washed. The intention was to use plaster for fireproofing the dwellings – a majority of which were timber with thatched roofs. The company seal bears the legend 'The Seal of the Art or Mystery of Daubers, now called Plaisterers, of the City of London'.

The Worshipful Company of Plumbers

Judging by one of the ordinances of the medieval plumbers' guild (around 1356), there was no place for what we now term cowboys. Plumbers had to be certified by the most skilful men in that craft so 'the trade might not be scandalised, or the commonalty damaged and deceived by folk who do not know their trade'.

The Worshipful Company of Poulters of London

Poultry was an important element of the medieval food supply and in 1274 a royal decree set the prices of twenty-two kinds of poultry. By 1299 the poulters were a recognised guild and in 1368 the company had the authority to regulate the sale of poultry, swans, pigeons, rabbits and small game. Today, the company is a charitable organisation that supports people in need, and funds education in poultry-related subjects.

The Worshipful Company of Saddlers

A guild of saddlers existed in 1160. At that time the horse was central to society. Today, the company is still involved with the trade by supporting trainee saddlers with bursaries and by promoting British equestrianism, focusing in particular on young and emerging riders.

The Worshipful Company of Scientific Instrument Makers

Early scientific instruments were made by blacksmiths, clockmakers and spectacle makers, but as science progressed with electronics and optics, a dedicated guild was formed to advance the profession. The company was granted livery status in 1964.

The Worshipful Company of Scriveners

Also known as 'the Mysterie of Writers of the Court Letter'. Scriveners are experts in writing legal documents. Since its foundation in 1373 the company has been responsible for examining, issuing qualifications and regulating full-time members of the profession of Scrivener Notary based in the City of London.

The Worshipful Company of Security Professionals

Few buildings in the City of London do not have some type of security, so in the traditions of the Square Mile those professionals now have a livery company that promotes their industry. This one was founded in 2008.

APPENDIX

The Worshipful Company of Shipwrights

London's pre-eminence as a trading port meant that shipwrights were rarely short of work. Written references date the guild to 1387, although it is thought to have existed before then. Over the years members from associated maritime professions joined the guild, including marine engineers, shipbrokers, naval architects and specialists in maritime law. Today the company supports maritime charities and education.

The Worshipful Company of Spectacle Makers

Like most London trade guilds, when it was founded in 1629 the Company of Spectacle Makers maintained standards in the profession. Company officers had the authority to search spectacle shops and if the goods were proved to be sub-standard the glasses were taken and ceremonially broken on London Stone, a chunk of rock in Cannon Street that is recognised as a symbol of the City. Today, the company oversees the training and examination of optical technicians.

The Worshipful Company of Stationers and Newspaper Makers

London's printing industry was historically centred on Fleet Street in order to serve the adjacent legal quarter and the religious orders around St Paul's cathedral. Britain's newspaper industry also grew up there, taking advantage of the skills that existed in the neighbourhood. Today the stationers' hall is still located in the area. The modern company is closely connected with a wide range of twenty-first century visual and graphic media industries.

The Worshipful Company of Tallow Chandlers

A guild was formed around 1300 by oynters (tallow melters) to regulate oils, ointments, lubricants and fat-based preservatives, and to manage candle-making using animal fats (tallow).

229

By 1415, tallow candles were used in the compulsory street lighting of London. Some current members of the company have direct links with the candle-making industry, including a company that crafts church candles.

The Worshipful Company of Tax Advisers
Formed in 2005 to promote the tax profession, this company provides tax briefings for the Lord Mayor when he is on official business overseas. He acts as an ambassador for the City and tax issues can influence whether an international company chooses to trade in London or not.

The Worshipful Company of Tinplate Workers
alias Wire Workers of the City of London
Early tinplate was used for drinking vessels, plates, bowls and lanterns. Wire objects included fishhooks, cages, chains and traps. The company was formed in 1670 as 'The Trade Arte and Mistery of Tynne Plate Workers als Wyer Workers of the City of London'.

The Worshipful Company of Tobacco Pipe Makers
and Tobacco Blenders
Well before Francis Drake introduced tobacco to England in 1586, English sailors had picked up the pipe-smoking habit from Spanish, Portuguese and French sailors. By 1613 there were over 7,000 'tobagies', or meeting houses, supported by the sale of tobacco. King James I was famously anti-smoking, allegedly describing it in words such as 'loathsome to the eye' and 'hateful to the nose'. But it was a lucrative source of tax revenue and so the king granted the company a charter in 1619.

The Worshipful Company of Turners of London
Turning is the craft of using a lathe to produce work with a rounded shape. Although there was a turners' guild in 1295, a

royal charter was not granted until 1604. St Catherine is patron saint of the turners, possibly because she was martyred on the Catherine Wheel and the wheel would have been partially crafted by a turner.

The Worshipful Company of Tylers and Bricklayers
The company's first royal charter was issued in 1568. Today, the membership rewards excellence in the crafts of bricklaying, applied wall and floor tiling, and roof tiling and slating with special awards, and supports many charities.

The Worshipful Company of Upholders
Upholder is an archaic word for a furniture upholsterer. They were first mentioned as an organised group in 1346 when they petitioned the king for protection against unfair competition from France. The upholders were recognised as a guild in 1360. Keen to protect the good name of their trade, they had the authority to destroy poorly made upholstery and to outlaw the use of materials other than properly treated feathers for stuffing and pillows.

The Worshipful Company of Water Conservators
The company was formed in 2000 and works to promote and spread awareness of the practice of water and environmental management. It is active in informing the government, the City and the public about the ways that water affects our lives. Membership is drawn from a number of environmental action groups.

The Worshipful Company of Wax Chandlers
Wax chandlers traded in beeswax products. Beeswax candles were customary in churches and to light the homes of the wealthy. Smelly tallow candles were used by everyone else. The wax chandlers' guild received its royal charter in 1484. The

company no longer has trade links with wax candle making but is a patron of the National Honey Show and the British Beekeeping Association.

The Worshipful Company of Weavers
This is the oldest recorded livery company with records dating to 1130. The weavers controlled production and marketing of woven goods at a time when textiles were England's premier export. Many of the company's latter-day members are involved in textiles and though it no longer regulates the industry, the company contributes to its survival with scholarships and awards.

The Worshipful Company of Wheelwrights
Making a carriage- or cartwheel by hand requires a great deal of skill. Creating a wheel that would withstand the pre-asphalt pot-holed roads and tracks was little short of a miracle. The work of wheelrights kept trade and people moving and the guild (formed in 1630) tried to ensure that wheels were not made of inferior materials that fell apart quickly.

The Worshipful Company of Woolmen
Woolmen were winders and packers of wool. Their guild was formed in 1180.

Wool exports helped England to prosper and the importance of the commodity was widely acknowledged, not least by Queen Elizabeth I, who supported the wool trade by ordering everyone over the age of six to wear a woollen cap on Sundays.

The Worshipful Company of World Traders
London has always been an international city with business links in dozens of countries. Membership of the Company of World Traders (founded 2000) is restricted to people who represent the global trading community in the City.

APPENDIX

The Worshipful Society of Apothecaries of London
The term 'apothecary' is derived from the Greek word *apotheke*, meaning storehouse. During the medieval era it was used to describe a person who traded spices and herbs. These often formed the basis of early medical treatments. In modern times, as a member of the United Examining Board, the company licenses doctors to practise medicine in England and Wales. It was founded in 1617.

Index of Customs
and Events

B

C

D

F

G

H

I

J

K

L

M

O

P

R

INDEX

W

www.summersdale.com